EXECUTIVE ACCOUNTABILITY

Creating the Environment for Business Value from Technology

Darlene Barrientos Crane and Margery Mayer

Westport, Connecticut
London

Library of Congress Cataloging-in-Publication Data

Crane, Darlene Barrientos, 1948–
    Executive accountability : creating the environment for business value from technology / Darlene Barrientos Crane and Margery Mayer.
        p.   cm.
    Includes bibliographical references and index.
    ISBN 1–56720–603–4 (alk. paper)
        1. Management—Data processing.   2. Information technology—Management.
3. Decision making—Data processing.   4. Management information systems.
5. Business enterprises—Communication systems—Management.   6. Capital
investments—Cost effectiveness.   I. Mayer, Margery.   II. Title.
        HD30.2.C72   2003
        658′.05—dc22   2003057977

British Library Cataloguing in Publication Data is available.

Library of Congress Catalog Card Number: 2003057977
ISBN: 1–56720–603–4

First published in 2003

Praeger Publishers, 88 Post Road West, Westport, CT 06881
An imprint of Greenwood Publishing Group, Inc.
www.praeger.com

Printed in the United States of America

The paper used in this book complies with the
Permanent Paper Standard issued by the National
Information Standards Organization (Z39.48–1984).

10 9 8 7 6 5 4 3 2 1

CONTENTS

PREFACE

WHY WE WROTE THIS BOOK

We wrote this book to assist executives in creating the business structure and organizational environment where management and staff are more innovative and effective in deriving measurable value from technology. Our goal is to share insights from advising and guiding companies in various industries through technology initiatives vital to long-term stability and growth. In addition, we present proven management principles and methods that allow companies to obtain value from technology as it continues to grow in processing power and functional capability.

When we signed the contract to write this book on September 30, 2001, we had a modest hope that many executives would realize that it was time to make significant improvements to decision making and management of technology. As we continued writing through the fall of 2002, many dramatic events occurred. There was a major downturn in the telecommunications industry, and massive corporate fraud surfaced. Executive accountability for the quality of operating management, ethics, and reporting led to greater regulatory review and penalties. As a result of these events, we became more proactive in defining processes and methods that can assist executives and their management teams in responding to these demands. All of the methods presented are based on those we implemented or realized were needed as businesses executed important technology initiatives. We are writing this book at the suggestion of our clients and graduate students who have encouraged us to share these methods with others.

THE AUDIENCE

The primary audience for this book is executives who realize that hype and hope from technology will neither satisfy investors nor help them address competitive business pressures. These executives want to take advantage of technology to increase organizational benefits and to secure long-term relationships with valued customers. They also want to minimize excessive costs and risks of financial losses and reduced productivity from failed or ineffectively managed technology initiatives. We are writing to those executives who are ready to take action.

As educators we realize a secondary audience is our graduate students. Our goal here is to contribute to the development of managers and working professionals into the next generation of business and organizational leaders. This book raises the questions and offers alternative recommendations to help current and future leaders better utilize technology to grow global markets and manage organizations. We hope that these leaders of business continue to improve organizational structure and processes to realize maximum value from technology investments.

METHODOLOGY OF THE BOOK

This book is the result of collaboration between a technology professional with a specialty in strategy and a business consultant with a specialty in business performance improvement, including technology and information use. The purpose of our collaboration is to encourage executives to think and act to generate business value from technology. The writing process involved one author writing a chapter from her specialty, then the other author reviewing and modifying it. This approach ensures that both the IT and business viewpoints are adequately and appropriately expressed. Our collaboration allowed us to create new processes and tools to allow executives to derive business value from technology.

The research process included one- to two-hour interviews with executives and managers to gather their experience with oversight and execution of technology investments. All of this material was used to create the foundation for this book. The stories written in the book are snapshots from the interviews or historical cases in our experience. When published sources are cited, references are given at the ends of the chapters.

ACKNOWLEDGMENTS

Many people were invaluable in helping us complete this effort. Nancy Southern assisted us with the book proposal and worked closely on the first few chapters. She shared her model of the cycle of blame and perspectives from an organizational change view. Steve Crane was our cheerleader, early editor on most of the chapters, and chef for tasty lunches on our writing days. Greg Diel and Ron Skelton were our readers for the first draft and provided us with great editing and comments. Jerry Talley, Rudite Emir, Marty Jordan, Michael Gray, and Sheila Sokel read selected chapters and provided helpful feedback and suggestions. Judith Maurier, our editor, was invaluable in helping us prepare the final manuscript.

We thank all of the people that shared their time to give interviews or add stories for our cases. Of course we appreciate our publishers and editors who encouraged us to do this work and offered suggestions to make it a valuable book.

INTRODUCTION

WHY YOU SHOULD READ THIS BOOK

Read this book to meet investor demands, improve your organization's business performance, and learn how to measure benefits from technology investments. Investors today are demanding that all capital investments be fully disclosed and that they deliver measurable business value to shareholders and customers. Because a significant portion of capital investments is for technology, a shift needs to occur from product thinking—in terms of purchases—to strategic thinking about technology to strengthen business performance. The shift means taking the right action at the right time on business opportunities and risks of technology investments. By taking the right action at the right time, a company can increase satisfaction and business results from customer interaction with technology. In addition, strategic thinking leads to identification of cost reduction and reduced organizational disruption from implementing technology. A comprehensive analysis of business readiness identifies risks of operating disruptions and their hidden costs. These risks can be minimized over the course of the investment. Meeting investor and customer demands requires that the organization and its business processes be designed to consistently generate value from technology investments. All of these changes to the organization cannot be accomplished without clearly specifying executive accountability for realizing the strategic value from technology.

Although this book is primarily directed to executives, those aspiring to leadership positions or interested in forming their own companies will discover that it can help them in designing future organizations that deliver value from technology investments. In the executive role there is pressure to make the right decisions about technology that support the growth and stability of the company. This book presents organizational issues, alternatives, processes, and actions that encourage strategic thinking and action to derive value from technology.

HOW TO GET THE MOST FROM THIS BOOK

To gain the most from this book, read it to find new ideas for thinking and acting to improve business performance and obtain strategic value from technology. Also consider how often your company is swayed by the myths of technology as opposed to its realities. Use this book to rethink investment strategies, plans, and capabilities of your organization to execute and achieve benefits from technology.

Each chapter presents an overview of a specific problem or way to improve the oversight and business results from initiatives. The heading, "What You Can Do" highlights specific actions your company can take. At the end of each chapter are questions to encourage further exploration of the topic and issues raised in obtaining value from technology investments.

Chapter 1: Debunking the "Promise of Technology." Use this chapter to move beyond the myths to the realities of value from technology investments. Identify the specific challenges organizations must overcome to achieve anticipated value. The lack of strategic thinking, unverified technology benefits, ineffective collaboration, vague management accountability, and oversight limit the results achieved from critical initiatives. Learn the steps needed to break through these challenges.

Chapter 2: Understanding the Victim's View of Technology. Compare your concerns and experiences from technology initiatives with others. Listen to the stories of technology's promises and its hard realities. Learn ways to find out if technology investments are successful and beneficial. Look for ways that frustration with technology can turn into a positive focus on value.

Chapter 3: Realizing the Strategic Value of Technology. See how other organizations apply technology to obtain strategic benefits. Examples of some well-known companies illustrate what you can do. An assessment is included that can assist your company in identifying its readiness to derive value from technology.

Chapter 4: Building Organization-Wide Processes for Delivering Value from Technology. Read four management approaches to deriving value from technology investments and determine which approach your company uses and understand its strengths and risks. Stretch your thinking by considering our model for executive, organization-wide, and local accountability for realizing business benefits from technology.

Chapter 5: Creating a Structure for Organization-Wide Collaboration. If better collaboration is needed among business, technology and management staff, read Chapter 5. It presents experiences from many major technology initiatives and shows how important collaboration is when the organization is under pressure to implement technology initiatives. The critical role of executives in establishing productive collaboration is also outlined.

Chapter 6: Developing Organization-Wide Technology Decision Making. To obtain options for improving decision making about technology and verifying benefits, go to Chapter 6. It shows how to better manage and identify important decisions that are frequently overlooked but necessary to achieve benefits. Tables present decisions necessary at the approval, in progress, and at completion of initiatives.

Chapter 7: Establishing a Value-Driven Management Process for Technology. Learn how to use The Seeing Solutions Map, a tested tool for fostering effective collaboration and managing technology from a business-value perspective. The tool illustrates how business and technology staff can better work together to identify and implement opportunities, reduce risks, and derive value from technology initiatives.

Chapter 8: Identifying the Value of Technology. Measuring the results from technology investments is difficult; Chapter 8 offers a way to start. Find out how the measurement of value from technology starts with the assessment and identifies critical areas where metrics and measurement apply. Learn the importance of high quality information necessary to make measurement reliable and valuable for business performance.

Chapter 9: Overseeing Initiatives to Generate Business Value from Technology. Executive oversight for initiatives is essential to deliver value from technology investments. Learn a new process—strategic initiative management—to provide appropriate oversight to fill the gap between strategic initiatives and the projects they generate. It's time to take accountability for the success of your technology initiatives.

Part I

MAKING THE CASE FOR CUSTOMER AND ORGANIZATION-WIDE BENEFIT FROM TECHNOLOGY

Chapter 1

DEBUNKING THE "PROMISE OF TECHNOLOGY"

The promise of technology is so powerful that executives assume it will propel a company to new heights of productivity, deliver customer satisfaction, and strengthen business performance. When technology is usable across the organization, it brings business and customer information to the fingertips of all staff. How do you know if these statements are true or not, and how does your company achieve these promises? In fact, confidence in benefits from technology remains surprisingly low. A recent survey showed that only 25 percent of chief executive officers are satisfied with the results they are obtaining from technology investments.[1] The perceptions of value received from technology are based on increasing direct involvement of executives with technology initiatives. In addition, executives are obtaining more information from subordinates on the effect of technology on operations and company performance. How can we close this gap between the promise of technology and executive satisfaction? Organization-wide oversight, management processes, evaluation criteria, and collaboration are more important than promises in driving technology initiatives. Your organization must know the difference between myth and reality regarding the ability to deliver measurable business benefit. Following are key myths about technology that must be turned into reality.

MYTHS AND REALITIES

Myth 1. I can purchase a technology product, install it, and realize tangible results quickly. Few technologies can be purchased, be easily implemented, and deliver quick business improvements. Technology usually takes time to implement, load with correct data, and integrate into existing business processes and systems. Often it requires new or modified business processes before it can be fully utilized and deliver benefits.

Myth 2. Technology alone will give me a competitive advantage. The reality is that technology must directly address a clear business need or opportunity for an organization to realize a competitive advantage and measurable benefit. How the technology is used to deliver customer value or additional productivity determines a company's competitive advantage.

Myth 3. Technology by itself generates positive changes in the way people work. It is true that technology will change how people work. But the new way of working with technology may or may not support business improvement. Too often technology is implemented without consideration of how it will affect staff, critical business operations, and overall business performance.

To determine the difference between myth and reality, one must identify technology's use and value to the business. In addition, the entire cost of implementing the technology, staff time, and the effects on the business must be identified and evaluated to realize actual benefits from these investments. Myths about technology benefits persist because the challenges of these investments are seldom articulated and addressed throughout the organization. Managers and staff who express frustration with technology are labeled as resistant to change or not supportive of management goals. In fact, many of these frustrations are really important concerns and challenges about how technology could affect business performance.

In this chapter we describe the challenges that must be overcome for executives to guide their companies to achievement of strategic and measurable business benefits from technology. The challenges we see are weak links between technology and strategic business objectives, unverified estimates of business benefits, hidden costs of implementation, ineffective collaboration, and vague management accountability and executive oversight.

CHALLENGES OF REALIZING VALUE FROM TECHNOLOGY

Lack of Strategic Thinking and Action about Technology

Projects are often managed as tactical actions to implement business objectives even though technology has the power to be a strategic resource. In this scenario, decision-making processes for technology focus on justifying a purchase for a project and allocating a budget. This approach limits consideration of all important business opportunities, risks, ramifications, and implications of technology to the organization and customers once it is implemented. Often middle managers who implement projects do not have access to business objectives, nor are they privy to changes in strategic direction. In the desire to rapidly purchase and implement technology, companies and vendors minimize or even eliminate assessment and analysis of current business processes and ignore how staff use technology to perform work. Risks associated with business operations are frequently minimized when organization-wide implementation of multiproduct technology solutions occurs.

After technology is purchased and projects are being implemented, decision makers focus on tactics and do not preserve the link between projects and business objectives. In many cases, technology projects take on a life of their own even when business conditions or objectives have changed and are no longer valid. Critical processes and checkpoints are often not in place to keep projects linked to strategy and objectives. There is no mechanism for redirecting or canceling projects after they have been initiated. The project managers and sponsors fight to keep projects alive even though their value may no longer be relevant.

Unverified Benefits and Business Cases for Technology

In the late 1990s, unverified benefits of technology were prevalent in business. Business cases were sometimes considered unnecessary constraints to getting the job done. Stories of technology decision meetings where managers with decision-making authority played electronic games on their personal digital assistants or chased an electric car around the floor were common. This frivolous approach to decision making is not based on any evaluation of business benefits. In a study of information systems and technology evaluation practices, the top two problems identified in structured technology evaluation were the identification and quantification of relevant benefits, occurring in 81 percent and 65 percent, respectively, of the projects studied.[2] Identification and quantification are essential to estimating relevant benefits from technology.

Classic financial formulas for technology purchases or project funding rely on accurate and reliable projections of cash flow, net profit, or other performance indicators. These formulas are only as good as the underlying assumptions and data used in the calculations. Technology staff and other analysts are skilled at finding business benefits that fit financial formulas to provide the return rates that result in a "yes" decision for a purchase. In many cases pressure to make a technology purchase quickly leads to financial projections with best case estimates of benefits. Often approvals of vendor proposals are completed before business initiatives are defined. This results in projects being launched prematurely and facts emerging later that change assumptions, scope, and estimates of benefits. When the technology implementation is finally completed, business process efficiency, service quality, and customer relationship improvements fail to materialize. Executives and staff are left wondering what business results actually were achieved after a successful technology implementation.

The risk of unverified benefit estimates is illustrated in a report of significant technology investments by the retail banking industry, which showed bank productivity actually decreased during the 1990s. The decrease was from 5.5 percent between 1987 and 1995 to 4.1 percent after 1995.[3] The largest investments in technology were for customer facing technologies designed to increase revenues. When the analysis of bank profitability realized from these investments was completed, 63 percent of the respondents answered "Don't Know" to the question, "What was the impact of customer-relationship-management sales tools on retail bank profitability?" The study did not indicate why the banks were willing to invest in these technologies without knowing about the actual business outcomes.

Assumptions of revenue generation from technology are often not based on actual measurement of customer use and benefit from technology. Many companies talk about improving the customer experience through technology, but do not invest in measurement and observation to improve their business or to design technology that customers use. In a recent study by the Patricia Seybold Group, 1,400 companies responded to a self-assessment on customer value and quality of experience. Companies in finance/banking and high tech scored about 3.80 on a scale of 1.80–4.00 on having a customer vision and strategy. This response shows a desire for customer focus. However, the same group of companies scored only 2.40 in actually measuring and managing customer value.[4] This means the companies did set a strategy but had little in place to measure customer experience and value. Another study by Patrina Mack, of about 50 smaller high tech companies showed that although they had customer information by segment, they were not able to identify their most profitable customers.[5]

Patrina Mack says that companies and executives make the choice to be customer focused or not. In addition, many marketing and sales staff believe they know their target market very well because they have constant contact with them. They do not realize that a lunch discussion with a customer does not always reveal specifics of the total customer experience, dissatisfaction, or needs for new products and services. Obtaining specific information from customers is essential to ensuring that products and services satisfy the marketplace and generate revenue.

When companies rely solely on vendors to analyze internal business needs and recommend appropriate technology, conflict of interest can be an issue, and the reliability of the information can be in question. Technology vendors know the standard benefits that can be derived from their products, and they look quickly at an organization to identify opportunities and to provide initial return on investment projections. However, vendors do not know the total costs or risks of these technologies to the company. Vendors typically want to avoid any information that will delay or add risk to a sale.

Outside consultants provide an independent evaluation of the benefits, risks, and costs of technology purchases to the business. Consultants use methods and tools they believe are useful. Companies must know if a consultant is using direct customer and end-user involvement or secondary sources to develop technology benefit estimates. Using primary business sources means that the consultant directly interacts with customers through interviews, focus groups, and/or surveys. Interviews could also be conducted with sales, service, and other customer facing staff to capture their views on needs and improvements in internal operations. Using secondary sources means the consultant obtains published information regarding population demographics and other data to make conclusions and recommendations. The company needs to determine if primary or secondary information supports estimates of benefits from technology. Companies must also know if the consultant uses methods and tools to support development of strategic thinking and action about technology. Without guidelines and checkpoints for the consultant, a company can end up with information that may or may not meet its needs.

Knowledge about how the business actually operates is useful in validating vendor and consultant estimates of benefits. However, the benefits identified by internal staff tend to be tactical and not strategic. If managers and staff do not have access to strategic plans and business objectives of the company and their business unit, then they are only able to consider limited functional improvements. When companies do not require staff to think more strategically, they limit the organization-wide benefits that could be achieved from technology.

The Challenges of Hidden Costs from Technology

The hidden costs from technology involve the total staff costs before, during, and after installation. It is time to stop dismissing these hidden costs as the "cost the business has to bear in implementing technology." There are hidden costs associated with using staff assigned to daily activities to work on technology projects. This means salary expenditures are not being used as budgeted for primary work tasks. The quality of the staff work for both responsibilities is reduced. This often leads to excessive overtime or to additional resources being needed to reduce operational work backlogs, research customer complaints, and correct errors.

A recent study, *The Hidden Cost of Software for the Contracting Organization,*[6] examined in detail the costs absorbed by companies purchasing large enterprise resource planning systems. The primary hypothesis of the study was that 50 percent of the organizations did not have a formal process for estimating the cost of their resources. The data showed that 88 percent of purchasing organizations did not estimate these hidden costs and only 25 percent included these costs in the economic analysis of the software technology. The startling statistic from the study was that these hidden costs were 190 percent (the mean value) of the software development costs, which occurred in business analysis, testing, and implementation. It is time for companies to begin to identify, track, and analyze direct and hidden costs of these technology investments. Often these hidden costs are high, therefore it is also important to look for all possible benefits from technology—both short and long-term—to offset them.

Challenges of Ineffective Collaboration about Technology

The importance of effective collaborative teams on producing good results from technology is discussed extensively in many articles and research studies. It is often a challenge to establish and maintain collaboration across organizations under the pressure of implementing technology investments. Staff still hesitate to collaborate when they encounter different work styles, challenging viewpoints, and strong political barriers. As technology has expanded across the organizational and global regions, staff from very different functions, backgrounds, and locations are expected to work together to meet very aggressive schedules. Under these conditions, introducing technology into organizations often accentuates existing vested interests, political barriers, and tensions. When an organization has rigid functional silos and inflexible professional groups, it is not clear how effective collaboration can be established as an organization-wide process. The groups try to meet and encounter difficulty in raising and resolving issues. When executives agree on what functions and professional groups must work together, productive collaboration can begin. If executives do not communicate a business need for organization-wide collaboration, then critical technology initiatives can be at risk.

Ineffective or nonexistent collaboration between business and information technology (IT) staff is sometimes the accepted practice in organizations. Business managers have budget control and often select technology and system integration consultants without involving the technology staff. Frequently, technology staff is discouraged from directly interacting with customers because marketing; sales, and service managers feel they should control all customer interactions. IT staff often make significant changes to the technology infrastructure or desktop systems and do not include business staff in selecting products or planning for implementation. This competition for control between business and IT functions actually reduces both groups' success. Researchers who studied this control issue discovered that corporate managers do not adequately assess and manage the tensions between the two groups."[7] Lack of communication between business and IT managers reduces the ability of technology to deliver value.

When executives do not to provide a good example of collaboration among the most senior management levels, organization collaboration for technology initiatives does not occur and is considered unnecessary. For example, in one of our turnaround assignments, a president and operations senior vice president of a large bank subsidiary had strong differences on how to manage technology. The president was primarily a sales and marketing executive and delegated technology to others. The senior vice president of operations was a turnaround specialist for the bank, assigned by corporate management to stabilize operations and systems after a painful technology implementation. He had a vision of introducing new technology to dramatically improve service, and he obtained corporate approval for a service improvement project using his long-term relationships with corporate executives. He never obtained the president's full support for the new technology. In addition, the president disliked the senior vice president's close relationship with corporate executives. Suddenly, when corporate management moved the senior vice president to another global region experiencing operational problems, the new customer service system initiative was halted. The president cancelled the project and brought in his own consultants. The technology project was being managed as a competition for power and not for customer value or operations productivity. Managers recognized that they had to support the president's technology project even if they saw no value to the business. This example shows how lack of collaboration between executives can result in ineffective technology and expenditures.

VAGUE MANAGEMENT ACCOUNTABILITY AND EXECUTIVE OVERSIGHT

Management accountability for technology and business improvement is often vague and fragmented. The following case illustrates how vague accountability across many business processes and functions leads to low-quality customer information and undermines efforts to improve product quality and staff productivity. A high-tech company was having problems measuring product reliability because the information they used was inaccurate. Product reliability problems were reported to the customer service center representatives, who used inconsistent and inaccurate procedures when entering the exact description of each product problem. In addition, customer service representatives were not the owners of the product reliability information; they only logged the complaints. The customer service system did not interface with the sales and financial systems. This caused the quality assurance function to manually adjust data from the customer service system to calculate monthly reliability statistics by product. The corporate quality manager was considered the owner of the product reliability data and was accountable for developing the reliability metrics and monthly measures by product. The vice president of product development, another function, did not have confidence in the product reliability statistics and frequently disputed the figures with the corporate quality manager. It became clear that this pattern of confused management accountability for product reliability and customer satisfaction had to be corrected after a downturn in sales occurred.

As a result of the need for maximum revenue, a task force was put together to improve information and product reliability statistics. However, discussions among the different functions dragged on because all parties were unsure who was actually accountable for developing and driving a solution. When the vice presidents finally made it clear to the task force that everyone needed to share information and cooperate to fix the problem, all groups began to work together productively. All the functions—quality assurance, product development, customer service, and sales operations—then revealed where the breaks in the product reliability process existed. The IT function provided the data to define and estimate a cost-effective solution. When an internal systems solution was completed, the quality function eliminated the manual analysis of product reliability statistics. The corporate quality assurance manager defined the data standards for customer service and the service organization agreed to use the standards. Product quality information was improved. This was a chaotic and reactive process at the time when the company needed to rapidly adjust to changing business conditions.

A NEW WAY OF THINKING ABOUT TECHNOLOGY IS NEEDED

A new way of thinking about technology is needed because technology touches everything in a company. Opportunities and challenges affect overall business performance—not just the success of individual projects. A few highly visible cases illustrate the connection between technology initiatives and business performance.

The first case that demonstrates the results of not identifying the effects of technology on business performance is the case of Hershey Foods Corporation. In the final months of 1999, the company could not deliver candy supplies to store shelves for Halloween, which is the single highest candy-consuming day of the year.[8] Three years earlier, the company began an initiative to upgrade software for its order entry, manufacturing, fulfillment, and delivery systems. The systems were completed in July of 1999, but by September of that year candy could not be shipped efficiently to customers, while inventory was piling up in the warehouses. In fact, the company was unsure if it could meet deliveries for the Christmas season. This problem became a front-page story in the *Wall Street Journal*, damaging Hershey's reputation. As a result, the net profit of Hershey Foods Corporation sank 19 percent in October 1999.[9]

An important reason for the problems with Hershey Foods Corporation's $110 million investment in technology was that the initiative included three different business technology products. SAP AG, Siebel Systems, Inc., and the Manugistics Group all provided technology and consultants. In addition, a new warehouse was being constructed. Even though all these efforts were implemented using project plans, the results did not allow Hershey to move candy from the warehouses to customers. Hershey did not have the processes to identify, analyze, and reduce the risks of running many parallel projects. Executives did not consider the total effect of these projects on the delivery of products at peak demand periods.

Mergers and acquisitions also demonstrate the necessity for a new way of thinking about technology. Identifying, planning, and executing a merger or acquisition is one of the most challenging business initiatives an organization can undertake. Frequently the integration of technology across the merging organization is the largest cost, highest priority, and most labor-intensive work effort of the merger. Often, in merger integration efforts, the resource demands and financial costs are vastly underestimated. The technology integration effort often becomes a huge project that is delegated to middle management with infrequent and unstructured oversight by executives. When this lack of executive oversight occurs, the expected benefits of the merger are negatively impacted. Too often the analysis of the processes necessary to conduct business and retain customers is not thoroughly completed. Technology changes are forced without adequate business analysis to know how risks of rapid implementation can be reduced. When disruption of mission-critical business functions occurs in financial industry mergers, customers often become dissatisfied and shift their business to competitors. Errors in providing products, services, and especially funds handling are usually what cause the customer to shift.

The merger of Wells Fargo Bank with First Interstate Bank in 1997 was a dramatic example of how technology integration affected the performance and value of the company. During that year, the *Los Angeles Times* reported that Wells Fargo Bank's stock fell 6.6 percent because of operations problems occurring after the merger integration was completed.[10] Customer deposits were actually posted to the wrong accounts, and as a result customer core deposits fell 7 percent. The company could not find the incorrectly posted money and did not reveal this error. They gave customers credit for the misplaced money, but it was too late; they lost customer confidence, resulting in closed accounts. The problem was an assumption that a prior successful merger with a much smaller bank (Crocker Bank) could be repeated. The First Interstate merger was a hostile takeover of a much larger bank with a very different culture and would require a unique integration process. The technology and operations integration between these two large banks was more complex and needed strong coordination, communication, and executive oversight.

Webvan offers another example of the need for clear management accountability and executive oversight. This startup company spent millions of dollars on technology without focusing on its customers' needs, buying patterns, and basic business practices.[11] The company built state-of-the-art warehousing and distribution technology. However, executives made incorrect assumptions about customer buying habits and about introducing the new technology and Web-based sales concept into the food distribution market. They also failed by not providing for multiple buying channels in addition to Web-based sales and because the food distribution industry has very low margins. To be profitable in food distribution, Webvan needed as many food distribution channels as possible and executives with experience in the industry. The business was never profitable, eventually had to declare bankruptcy, and was liquidated. An analysis of the Webvan case in the *Wall Street Journal* cautioned, "Don't offer consumers a new technology unless it solves their problems better than their current solution." Executive accountability for doing thorough investigation into the food industry as well as the technology was lacking. This is an expensive example of the lack of clear management accountability and oversight.

WHAT YOU CAN DO: INTRODUCE ORGANIZATION-WIDE STRATEGIC THINKING AND ACTION

A first step to developing clear organization-wide accountability for initiatives where technology is an integral component is strategic thinking. This new way of thinking is not solely the responsibility of executives. It should occur at all levels to support the mission, goals, and objectives of the organization. Managers at all levels need to think strategically in order to help the organization achieve its goals. Typically, managerial thinking focuses on sustaining stability, the position the company holds in the market, and future steady growth. Strategic thinking encourages the organization to cross barriers and functional silos to focus on what is needed for the entire business and not merely on the needs of one department or business line.

This book defines strategic thinking as considering all the possibilities, opportunities, risks, and value that technology offers the business. Strategic thinking should occur in the normal course of doing business and especially when managers meet to recommend, launch, and implement technology. Strategic thinking about technology and the business should be part of monthly, quarterly, and annual business reviews. We find that more companies are beginning to realize that strategic thinking is essential to achieve a competitive advantage. Strategic thinking allows staff to see how they contribute to company value and encourages them to be more connected to the company objectives.

Many companies do not encourage their staff to think strategically, nor do they realize the benefits strategic thinking can deliver. Many technology initiatives start off well but then get bogged down in the detail and take on a life of their own. Staff often focus on a particular tactical result and lose track of the strategic purpose, changes in the marketplace, and results that must be realized at the time the initiative is complete. They are often so driven by management to deliver projects rapidly and with few resources that they cannot even attempt to think strategically. When employing strategic thinking and driving technology initiatives, executives must reinforce business outcomes consistently with managers.

Table 1.1 illustrates how strategic planning is different from strategic thinking. Strategic planning is the formal business process of defining long-term and annual business plans. Executives, advisers, and the management team support the research, analysis, and definition of the vision, values, and mission that drive the company. The high-level statements are translated into specific strategic initiatives for implementation. This process is typically top-down driven and may be a general call to action or be supported by detailed implementation processes linked to each individual's performance plan. In contrast to strategic planning, strategic thinking is continuous across the organization. Strategic thinking requires management to consider sustaining and growing the value of the company in every short-and long-term effort. Managers consider how each work effort could deliver value to the business.

To introduce strategic thinking to a company, executives must first define it as a high-priority initiative. The scope of strategic thinking responsibility for each level of management should then be clarified. A strategic thinking initiative can then be implemented through training or by using it within specific projects.

SUMMARY

Executives must learn to think in a new way in order to build the organization structure, management processes, and methods that will al-

Table 1.1
Strategic Thinking versus Strategic Planning

Strategic Thinking: Considering Possibilities	Strategic Planning: A Call to Action
Continuous process across the organization	Annual event
Focus on generation of value	Top-down process
Deliver on core value proposition of the company	Translate strategies into implementation
Link strategies and objectives to programs and projects	Organization may be working with the strategy
Connect day to day activities to achieving longer-term objectives	Daily activities not always focused on achieving strategic objectives

low them to move beyond the myths of technology to realize measurable value. As the power of technology grows, challenges remain that constrain organizations from realizing its value. The challenges include lack of strategic thinking about technology, inadequate analysis of needs, unverified benefits, hidden costs, ineffective collaboration, and confused accountability and oversight for business results. To overcome these challenges, a new way of thinking about technology must include an organization-wide view that links business objectives, initiatives, and tactical technology projects. Introducing ongoing strategic thinking at all levels of the organization is an important step in shifting your company to this new way of thinking.

QUESTIONS FOR REFLECTION AND DISCUSSION

1. Does your company have a strategic plan that outlines technology's measurable value to the company?

2. How are business strategies, objectives, and initiatives linked to projects?

3. How are business benefits of technology verified with information from customers and staff?

4. If the IT-business gap exists at your company, how does it affect results from technology?

5. What checkpoints and processes do you have to prevent technology implementation challenges that affect business performance?

6. What can your company do to overcome the challenges of realizing value from technology?

NOTES

1. Tallon, P., K. Kraemer, and V. Gurbaxani. "Executives' Perceptions of the Business Value of Information Technology: A Process-Oriented Approach." *Journal of Management Information Systems* (Spring 2000): 145–174.

2. Ballantine, J., Galliers, R, and Stray, S. "Information Systems, Technology Evaluation Practices." *Beyond the IT Productivity Paradox.* Chichester: John Wiley & Sons, 1999, p. 142.

3. Olazabal, N. G. "Banking: The IT Paradox." *McKinsey Quarterly* 1, no. 1 (2002); available from Proquest database archives, p. 1 of 4.

4. Aldrich, S. "Where Do We Stand on Customer Value & QCE?" Reported by Patricia Seybold Group's, Strategic Planning Service. 14 March 2002, Illustration 1.

5. Mack, P. "After Internet Time: 5 New Realities for Product Development in the Internet Economy." Report by Vision & Execution, Menlo Park, CA, 2002.

6. Haddad, M. *The Hidden Cost of Software for the Contracting Organization.* Dissertation for American University (Washington, D.C., September 1999).

7. Kettinger, K., and C. Lee. "Understanding the IS-User Divide in IT Innovation." *Communications of the ACM* 45 (February 2002): 79–90.

8. Nelson, E., and E. Ramstad. "Trick or Treat: Hershey's Biggest Dud Has Turned Out to Be Its New Technology: At the worst possible time, it can't fill its orders, even as inventory grows." *Wall Street Journal,* October 29, 1999, pp. 1–4.

9. Branch, S. "Hershey Net Sinks to 19%; Snafus Linger," *Wall Street Journal,* October 26, 1999, pp. 1–2.

10. Vrana, D. "Merger Woes Take Toll on Wells Fargo: Stock falls 6.6% after firm says quarterly earnings again won't meet *Wall Street* estimates. First Interstate takeover cited." *Los Angeles Times,* July 10, 1997, pp. 1–3.

11. Blackwell, R. "Manager's Journal: Why Webvan Went Bust." *Wall Street Journal,* July 16, 2001, pp. 1–2.

Chapter 2

UNDERSTANDING THE VICTIM'S VIEW OF TECHNOLOGY

"Business managers learn by being victims of enterprise resource planning projects." This was a project director's explanation of how he learned to manage a $20 million technology initiative. His response was intense but familiar, so we decided to devote an entire chapter to the victim's view of technology. Here we illustrate how technology is often blamed for project failure, and we discuss how vital it is to know the real issues and to take appropriate action to resolve these for technology to be successful.

The anecdotes in this chapter illustrate the profound effect of technology on the entire organization. This effect can be called a cycle of blame[1] that originates from unarticulated frustration surrounding technology. Understanding the cycle of blame is key to making changes to roles, responsibilities, and actions that will allow companies to derive business benefits from technology. Executive action is often necessary to verify the underlying problems and establish processes for resolving the use and value of technology. The bottom line is that this frustration—the cycle of blame—cannot be ignored.

Before the organization can begin to refocus on improvement and benefits from technology it is important for staff to voice current frustrations. As this happens, a picture of who controls the technology business proposals, who makes the decisions, and who manages the processes is revealed. In working with organizations, one of our first steps is to listen to frustrations and concerns so that we can determine the effects of technology on the business. In interviews we often find that executives, managers, and other staff are all negatively affected by technology or the processes and projects related to it. Many feel there is no mechanism for articulating that no process exists for sorting through difficult situations before business problems occur. As the frustration grows, just hearing the word "technology" often draws a cautious or negative response. In this chapter, we illustrate a cycle of blame that affects executives, management, staff, and the company's value from technology. We focus on how to shift thinking from blame to innovation and opportunity. Finally, we suggest what you, the executive, can do to encourage this new thinking.

THE CYCLE OF BLAME

Victim behavior is both the cause and effect of the cycle of blame. When the cycle takes hold in organizations, strong individual beliefs are formed that inhibit accountability and effective action. When people do not believe they have the ability to achieve desired results and will be blamed for any failure, they feel powerless and become victims. Powerlessness fuels mistrust, which causes strained relationships and often sabotage. When mistrust prevails, avoidance of communication and ineffective negotiations and decisions among divisions become an expected pattern. Without effective relationships focused on mutual benefit, no one can produce the desired results. Over time, this behavior forms a pattern of blame that has a detrimental effect on the organization. Even though people may be doing their best, their inability to produce results often causes others to believe that they do not have the best interests of the organization in mind. Sometimes this is true. Often people begin to take more independent action, doing what they believe is best to protect themselves and their positions. Their actions may or may not be what is best for the organization.

We found that the victim's view is strong among business managers and technology staff as well. Often IT project managers view themselves as targets because they have responsibility with no authority to deliver successful technology projects with business benefits. They might also believe that they are victims of the business organization's constant demands for completing projects faster with fewer and fewer resources. Organizations assume that IT staff are accountable for making projects successful, even when the business units do not contribute the requisite resources. For example, often business staff cannot take the time to define business requirements. Project delivery dates are announced without addressing the added risk to existing work, systems, and quality. If the project fails to deliver the required results, the IT department is blamed and the cycle of blame begins.

How the Cycle of Blame Affects the Application of Technology in Business

The following anecdotes illustrate the victim's view and how the cycle of blame takes hold, causing technology investments and projects to fail.

Case 1: Where Was the Accountability?

Let's look at an example where the lack of accountability led to an organization-wide cycle of blame. A medium-sized technology company launched an initiative to improve the sales forecasting and fulfillment processes. The president said it "had to happen!" A multimillion-dollar budget was approved and the project progressed for months without any-one ever defining, documenting, and validating the business require-ments. As a result, the scope of the project kept shifting and growing. The president took little ownership of the initiative and did not require executive reviews. Nor did he understand the effect this lack of account-ability had on achieving company results. Accountability for the project was delegated to the executive vice president of operations, who was not known for being an assertive leader. Responsibility for the project was given to the project director and fulfillment managers.

The project director, who was responsible for delivering technology to improve the fulfillment process, felt powerless because there was no strong executive support. The effort was viewed merely as an operations project. There was little accountability even though this project employed expensive external consultants and affected sales, fulfillment, and IT. Sales forecasting staff participated in the project, but there was no spon-sor from the sales organization to lobby for their needs. The president and executive vice president did not establish an oversight process with triggers for escalation to keep the initiative progressing.

When we run this case through the cycle of blame filter, we can see that everyone involved with the effort was frustrated and eventually be-gan blaming one other for the stagnating project that was supposed to be a high priority. The IT organization and the external consultants were fearful of being blamed and tried protecting themselves. Both the project director and the business team, mistrustful of IT and the external con-sultants, were also fearful of being blamed. Executive management was unaware of the importance of clear accountability for this multimillion-dollar project and was fearful that the project was out of control. The operating staff found themselves responsible for producing business results without sponsorship or direction. There was no process to present their issues or needs and obtain a business decision based on how best to proceed with the project. Everyone in this case was caught in either avoiding blame, finding someone to blame, or working with high levels of mistrust and frustration.

What can be learned from this case? The situation could be improved only with the president's involvement, support, and oversight. The project needed to be a high priority, requiring executive time and oversight. If the project did not warrant executive time and oversight, then it should have been cancelled and the budget reallocated. Accountability needed to be clarified for each function involved in the effort. There should have been a way for issues and frustration to be vocalized constructively, for changes to be identified earlier, and for the project's likelihood of delivering business benefits that exceed the cost and effort expended to be evaluated constantly.

Case 2: The Users Won't Use It!

Let's consider an executive-launched initiative to provide a Web-based technology system to take staff recruitment for a healthcare organization to new levels of speed and efficiency. The goal was that hiring managers would be responsible for the entire recruitment effort using an improved state-of-the-art system. Throughout the project, data accuracy was a problem, causing a high level of dissatisfaction with staff. Unfortunately, hiring managers were not involved in the project planning, and there was little communication from the executive sponsor of this technology initiative to prepare them for their added responsibilities for recruitment. When they realized there would be additional work with the new system, they balked at using the technology because they had no input into system design. Furthermore, staff were not trained in how to use the system, and it was severely underutilized. The hiring manager and staff blamed IT for not delivering a quality product that reduced their workload and provided value. IT blamed senior management for not providing the sponsorship and support needed for a successful implementation. The cycle of blame was everywhere.

What is important about this case? Executives were unaware that their lack of communication to managers about the impending changes caused the low usage. For this system to work effectively, the existing process and steps for resumes, candidates, interviewing, selecting, and hiring needed to be fully understood and then modified for the new technology. Technologists were unable to conduct this analysis, design, and evaluation without management and staff involvement. When detailed analysis and observation of the actual workflow was overlooked, there was little real information to develop effective systems and improved processes. Early participation with the design of the system was key in making it "user friendly" and a vital part of staff work. It is important for managers and staff to be exposed to new technology early in the implementation process in order to assess whether or not the technology will work and whether or not the target audience will use it. Until organizations realize how critical identifying current work processes are, systems will continue to be underutilized, hampering business effectiveness and wasting precious capital.

Case 3: Victim of the Vendor

A third case is provided by a major insurance company replacing the existing client policy reporting system with a new, faster, more efficient technology engine. The business case presented to the president promised tremendous return on investment and global expansion opportunities, such as Web access and customer query capability, all needed to keep up with competition. He approved it, the system specifications were written, an outside software development company was hired, and the project began.

It was well underway when an issue with the software development company arose. The vendor stopped work and demanded more money to complete the project to specifications. The vendor blamed the insurance company staff for not writing specific enough requirements; the staff blamed the vendor for not estimating correctly and falling behind schedule. They resolved their differences and the project continued.

The work progressed until the user-training phase when the staff discovered that the system did not always work and was very slow. They could not complete any inquiries before the system shut down completely. When the vendor was notified of the problems it stopped the project and demanded additional capital to continue. The vendor and insurance company negotiated the cancellation of the remaining contract. The source code was released, and development continued in-house at the insurance company until the project was successfully completed.

What is important about this case? The president felt powerless and victimized by the vendor. The vendor felt it was a victim of this very complex project and blamed the insurance company for not providing complete enough specifications. All key parties were more concerned with placing blame than they were with moving beyond blame. This case is typical of what can happen when buyers and vendors of software products do not have a clearly defined relationship, an agreement of the full scope of work, and a process to identify and resolve differences.

Case 4: The Product Manager As Victim

The project for a new service was initiated by the advanced technology function of a telecommunications company. At the time, the company did not have a marketing department and the project had been launched without any validation of customer needs. A financial analyst from corporate development had created a business case based on internal company assumptions. To implement the new service, IT changes to the billing system were required. The project was launched with an estimated budget of $100,000 for IT expenses. The overall budget rapidly ballooned and the project soon lost its way. Senior management appointed a product manager from the newly formed marketing department to get the project back on track.

The product manager conducted a market trial, which proved that assumptions about customer requirements and the business case were invalid. The business case assumed that the target customer was a heavy user of cell phones. When the product trial was conducted, the results indicated that the light-to-medium-level cell phone user was more interested in the product than the heavy user. The medium-level user was very cost-containment oriented and wanted to reduce incoming cell phone calls.

When the IT function estimated the final budget to modify the billing system to support the new service, the budget had grown to $1 million. The IT function believed these costs were not worth the benefit and deferred its concerns about the budget to executive management. The project was finally cancelled and the product manager who was called in to save the project was targeted as a problem.

Victims in this case are the product manager, customers, and investors. The product manager was called in to save a product development project that was formed on weak business assumptions and subject to ineffective coordination across business functions and reactive executive oversight. The product manager was asked to save a product development project that should never have been launched. The company executives, corporate business planning, and IT focused on finding blame for the failure of the product development effort rather than defining and validating the right product concept and target market. Executives needed to establish a formal marketing function to support the rapid growth of the company. Investors were victims because the capital they contributed was not used in the most productive manner. Customers also were victims because those who could benefit from a product tailored to medium-use levels did not have their needs met.

Breaking the Cycle of Blame and Eliminating Victim Behavior

It is possible to break the cycle of blame. Here is an example of how a vice president of E-business for a financial services firm, having decided to stop the cycle of blame, made both IT and the business organization responsible for results from technology projects. The first step she took was to listen to both the business and IT staffs' frustrations.

Her efforts began with a project that involved Website reporting for financial managers. Its goal was to reduce the use of paper, decrease costs, and increase the query and analysis capabilities of the reporting system. When reviewing the usage statistics, she found that the system was underutilized and did not deliver the expected cost savings. This was troublesome because she had been the executive sponsor and was convinced that savings could be achieved. She began by interviewing the financial managers as to why they were not using the new system. They told her that they did not attend the technical training classes and the system seemed cumbersome; they blamed IT for installing an unworkable system. She discovered through interviews that IT staff were frustrated by the complaints from the managers who spoke of the complexity while refusing to attend training. Using this information, she initiated a communication and training program to increase usage of the Website. She gave both groups three months to either use it or turn it off. After three months, she checked usage statistics and found that the Website was a regularly used tool.

The vice president used this project as a way to create a partnership between the two units for customer benefit. She diffused the desire to blame by replacing it with a focus on finding a long-term improvement for company benefit. A process improvement partnership between the two units was developed and piloted. The vice president further helped draft the following principles for building relationships surrounding technology investments and commitments from both business and technology.

Joint Principles for Collaboration

- Technology and business staff jointly identify solutions and set priorities.
- Technology, process, and implementation decisions are shared.
- Technology is used with other tools for business solutions.
- Mutual understanding, respect, and open communication surrounding technology are essential.

After the principles of the partnership were established the process for achieving them was defined. Each business initiative had an IT person working with operating staff regarding the business impact of technology change. Because the groups had clearly defined roles, approval levels, skills, and commitment, the cycle of blame was dramatically reduced.

The vice president reinforced partnerships among the three management functions reporting to her: program, business, and technical project managers. Each had a well-defined responsibility and role in contributing to the success of projects. Teaming diverse groups is not new, but making them jointly responsible for the ultimate results and measuring their success is new. Requiring that all groups stay involved before, during, and after the project is completed ensures that the technology will be better accepted and its benefits realized. The teaming approach must be supported at an executive level and built into the hiring practices, incentive plans, and development plans for all business and IT managers. Then long-term relationships can be built and utilized during technology projects to avoid the cycle of blame and to focus on a commitment to results.

The Shift in Thinking: From Victim to Innovation and Opportunity

When executives are committed to supporting the effective application of technology for achieving business results, they create the possibility for a new operating culture where leaders, team members, and key stakeholders focus on innovation and opportunity for mutual benefit. This new approach requires a shift in thinking from "What's in it for me?" to "What can we create together that will benefit the whole organization in delivering value to customers?"

Another product development director from Case 1, "Where Was the Accountability?" was aware of the need for executives to shift their thinking. He believed that the technology products created were more sophisticated than the business's capability to apply the applications to derive maximum value. The director commented that a company that buys packaged software must consider how the entire organization needs to change if is going to exploit the software's capabilities and generate value. In addition, coordination and collaboration must occur over the entire implementation to meet business objectives. Organizations need executive oversight and communication to make the right decisions about technology and its use. IT staff also must recognize that the issues and needs of business functions and customers should affect the selection, design, and implementation of technology.

WHAT YOU CAN DO: CHANGE HOW THEY THINK

The following table represents current viewpoints and how they must change to support company goals through successful technology initiatives. The first column of Table 2.1 describes the current thinking regarding technology by key job roles typically involved in technology initiatives. The second column describes the new thinking necessary to discover and implement strategic business opportunities from technology.

Important shifts in thinking are described in this table. First, the system designer shifts from protecting and controlling specifications to including the business in this process. Executives sponsoring technology initiatives shift from avoiding a failed technology effort to applying their authority to resolve issues and produce results. Middle managers shift from fear of technology projects to assuming business accountability for the results. End users shift from reluctance to use technology to a proactive role in voicing concerns and identifying requirements for using technology to improve their work.

Some effects of this shift in thinking are not as direct. An example is a sponsoring executive trapped by the cycle of blame. He has limited funds and many technology initiatives to complete, so he arbitrarily allocates budget, which underfunds some projects. His logic is that if an underfunded project fails, he can claim he did not waste budget. Conversely, if it succeeds, he could claim that the initial estimates were inflated and he was wise to hold the budget down. Arbitrary allocation places underfunded projects in a situation where they are set up to fail because they are launched with inadequate resources to deliver business results. Shifts in thinking are required before all groups can begin to think of opportunities to support the business instead of ways to deflect blame.

Table 2.1
Cycle-of-Blame Thinking versus Strategic Opportunity Thinking

	Thinking Trapped by the Cycle of Blame	Thinking Open to Strategic Opportunity
System Designer:	I want to limit and control the specifications because I don't trust users to know how to develop detailed and stable requirements.	We have a process to share our knowledge, concerns and obtain decisions that support useful systems.
Operating Manager:	I need a new system and I don't trust the IT department but I'm still dependent on them.	I manage operations daily and have an identified partner in IT who is prepared to work with me to apply his/her technical expertise.
Sponsoring Executive:	My rewards and bonuses are not tied to company performance. I don't want to put my name on this project until I know it won't hurt my career.	I am accountable for creating an environment to deliver a result to the company. I will apply my authority to make the decisions and create the environment where initiatives and staff produce results.
End Users:	I know I need a better system, but I am afraid that the resulting system makes my job harder. How do I know the impact a new system will have on my work?	I have a way to communicate my concerns and explain my work to the project staff. If there is a negative impact to my job I'm not surprised. Implementers will tell me early. I know my manager has a responsibility to produce a positive outcome.
Project Manager:	I must narrow the scope of the project so that we are on time and on budget and my job is safe.	I know how to achieve business value from projects. I define this project and understand how I must work with others to deliver a benefit to the sponsor and company.
Peer Managers:	That department is starting a project. They have always failed in the past. I just want to stay as far away as I can from that effort.	That department is starting a project. I can share ideas and make suggestions to avoid past mistakes. We all need to work for the benefit of the company.
Vendors:	I just want to sell this product and get my commission. Then I can turn it over to consultants and let them take any hits.	I understand how to help customers with measurable results. I want to get this sale and keep a relationship that is mutually beneficial.
Investors:	I have concerns about the value of the company. The track record for projects is not good. Maybe I should sell my technology stock.	This company has a high rate of success for new technology initiatives and gets excellent results. I'll buy the stock!

WHAT YOU CAN DO: GATHER CONTINUOUS FEEDBACK

We recommend that companies establish a mechanism to break the cycle of blame by gathering feedback from customers and staff regarding their frustrations with technology, using the following steps.

- Conduct usage surveys after every new technology system is implemented.

- Interview key staff and customers after system changes.

- Conduct an on-line survey to gather satisfaction information.

- Analyze results from these studies to identify the most important issues.

- Develop action plans to increase customer satisfaction.

SUMMARY

Voices of frustration need to be heard before staff can shift their attention to solving problems and creating new business opportunities utilizing technology. Listening to these frustrations and concerns about technology is critical to taking the first step in increasing business results from technology. Do not minimize the power of the cycle of blame to disrupt business performance and benefits from technology investments. Our stories illustrate that executives, technologists, business staff, and managers are all frustrated at times with technology and poorly managed initiatives. In later chapters you will find alternatives for moving your organization beyond the cycle of blame.

QUESTIONS FOR REFLECTION AND DISCUSSION

1. How often do you hear that results from technology investments are late or never realized?

2. How do staff feel when new technology is implemented?

3. Who participates in defining requirements, making decisions, and implementing technology projects?

4. Have staff voiced issues and concerns before and, if so, what were they?

5. Who drives the technology decisions in your company, and what are the effects on others not in the decision process?

6. How is the accountability for success communicated?

7. Who is ultimately responsible when technology does not meet expectations and deliver value?

8. How do staff understand the business effect of technology implementation?

9. What can you do to reduce wasted energy and promote more partnering for value from technology investments?

NOTE

1. Southern, N. "The Cycle of Blame." Unpublished paper. San Ramon, California, 2002:1.

Chapter 3

REALIZING THE STRATEGIC VALUE OF TECHNOLOGY

Realizing that technology is the digital nervous system of any business is the first step in understanding its strategic value. Strategic IT is the way technology is used for business benefit that gives it strategic and competitive advantage. It includes all hardware, telephone, desktop computer, cell phone, electronic organizer, software, database, cabling, network, and supporting technologies. Supporting technologies are transparent or invisible and allow anywhere, anytime access and utilization. When technology is strategic it produces vital information that allows executives to make decisions that could make or break a company. It is vital to keeping businesses alive and growing.

What would happen if all electronic devices, phones, and computer systems stopped? Business would be disrupted. Employees and customers would have to conduct businesses manually. This scenario would be bleak for many companies that totally rely on technology to conduct business. In this chapter we identify how technology fits into corporate strategy and how it is essential to a company's success. We begin by identifying the strategic value of technology and offer examples of companies that view their technology as strategic. Next, we explore how to evaluate whether a company uses technology strategically. This chapter concludes with a discussion of the importance of executive ownership for realizing the strategic value of technology investments—even if the actual tactical decision making and execution is delegated to others.

Let's begin by reviewing where technology fits into corporate strategy—the set of goals, objectives, and policies that guide the company. Technology supports these goals, objectives, and policies by providing the physical link for all company business. The strategic value of technology comes from the capabilities it provides to improve company performance, reach new markets, and seize business opportunities through productivity gains and customer satisfaction. This is achieved through faster access to vital information and improved company responsiveness. Vital technology can uniquely position a company in its market by supplying information for fast-paced change or strategic moves. It is "the enabling foundation of shared information technology capabilities upon which business depends."[1] Technology delivers strategic value when it speeds up operational efficiency and allows customers to easily access company information.

Strategic technology provides vendors, customers, and service providers with secure access to company products, services, and other resources bypassing gatekeepers and slow manual processes. Figure 3.1 illustrates how internal staff are mobilized immediately to respond to fully automated inquires and orders. For example, supply chain technology allows for up-to-the-minute information, which identifies the minimum product inventory levels needed to meet customer demand. Vendors and service providers often access a company's network as well, making the technology infrastructure even more critical or strategic. Adding Internet capability with secure transactions to protect information expands staff, supplier, and customer access to sales and service from anywhere in the world.

Many companies utilize technology in this way but do not realize its strategic importance and potential contribution. Technology can eliminate the three-to-six part documents that are manually reviewed, repackaged, and circulated for approval. Today's technology electronically circulates a document to all parties at the same time, eliminates the linear process, and delivers the transaction information instantaneously for review and approval. The shift from linear handoffs to instantaneous access pushes the responsibility for action to staff. The efficiencies achieved from this can increase revenue and reduce per-transaction costs significantly. A few years ago a major bank purchased technology to replace their multipart forms with electronic workflow systems. Before the bank changed to this system it processed 10 loans per week. After the change it processed 10 loans per day.

Companies can affect market perceptions by how they utilize and showcase technology. Retail chains can reach a new and younger audience by utilizing other delivery channels such as compelling Website

Figure 3.1
Strategic Technology

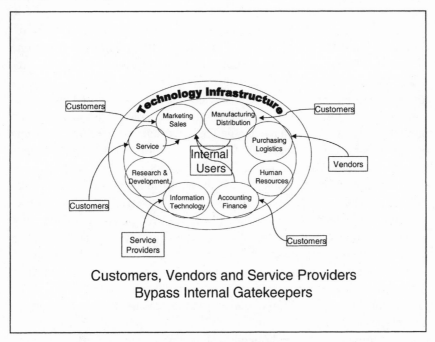

**Customers, Vendors and Service Providers
Bypass Internal Gatekeepers**

technology and in-store multimedia to increase sales. Technology can improve a company's reputation, position, differentiation, and leadership. For example, The Territory Ahead began as a catalog retailer of women's high-end clothing and became a Web-based retailer as well. Both the catalog and Website were so attractive, engaging, and easy to use that sales grew and the company built a strong and loyal customer base. The cash flow and popularity supported the opening of stores in high-end shopping centers. This company is a good example of how technology supported the company objectives and grew its market position.

For companies to realize the strategic value from technology, technology must produce measurable benefits. Examples of benefits that can be derived from technology include productivity improvements, up-to-the-minute inventory management, and customer service self-help from a Web-based enterprise-wide application. General Motor's enterprise-wide SAP implementation delivers real-time financial information to help the company meet customer demands and ensure its market leadership. The company spends over $200 million for technology annually to hold its market position. Chief Information Officer Ralph J. Szygenda involves the chief economic officer in critical technology decisions and requires that all technology investments deliver measurable value to the company.[2]

Technology is now critical to meet competitive pressures. FedEx recently received the Chief Information Officer 100 Award for being one of the best-applied technology companies in the country. FedEx has realized the strategic value of technology in its market position and customer retention. FedEx literature states, "The IT strategy of FedEx is to continue its improvement of technology to enable customers, to gain market share, and to improve efficiency through pioneering electronic commerce and supply-chain solutions."[3] Its major competitor, UPS, also uses technology. UPS literature states, "Technology is a means to increase connectivity, to enhance collaboration, and to drive efficiencies that will enable our company to be more responsive and competitive." The fierce competition between FedEx and UPS caused both companies to invest in Internet-driven logistics systems that can track an order from the time it is picked up through its journey in real time. FedEx's and UPS's technology advances have caused the US Postal Service to follow their lead and invest in logistics technology. These companies will have to continue to invest in innovative technology to secure competitive advantage.

Technology can change how customers engage with an entire industry. American Airlines dramatically changed how customers book travel. It was the first airline to offer Internet based "E-tickets" that allow passengers to plan and purchase tickets efficiently, and often at reduced cost.[4] This technology resulted in value from cost savings, by increased Web-based ticketing, and reduced travel agent fees and travel desk staff. American Airlines set the technology standard, and now almost all commercial airlines encourage Web-based ticketing. In 1996 American Airlines created Sabre, a legal entity, and offered the stock to the public for the first time. With popular acceptance of the Internet, they created Travelocity.com as their trademark Web-based ticketing site.

Other less global companies also take advantage of their strategic technology investments. Limited Brands, a conglomerate of Express, Lerner NY, The Limited, Henry Bendel, Victoria's Secret, and Bath and Body Works, is a retailer that values its Just-In-Time technology systems for sales order tracking to ensure that the right products are in the stores at the right time. The Limited Web site states that "Through the innovative applications of technology, business process, and information" the company creates shareholder value and meets customer expectations.[5] Valuing the technology's strategic advantage was one factor that allowed this conglomerate to grow so dramatically in the past five years. InStratnet, a marketing and logistics company, recently installed and is deriving value from customer relationship management. David Anderson, managing director said, "Think of the opportunities this 'one stop' information resource has on the company." It allows InStranet company-wide access to buying habits and trends of customers for better decisionmaking and timely product development. This truly delivers strategic value from technology.

Here are some questions for executives and staff to determine whether or not technology is strategic and providing value.

- How does technology support a strategic initiative or business objective? Every technology investment should prove that it supports strategic initiatives and objectives. There must be links to a strategic initiative or objective for every technology- and business-related project.
- How can I determine if a technology meets our business goals and objectives? Any technology investment must have measurement criteria tied to business goals and objectives that are periodically reviewed.
- What does our technology do to make us more competitive? You must know how your competitors are using technology. Then compare your use of technology to that of your competitors. Finally, determine what customers will be demanding in the future and identify your technology plans to stay competitive.
- How will I know if a technology initiative helped gain competitive advantage? You must take your measurement criteria created at the outset of the initiative and compare it to the result after the technology is implemented. The change from estimated benefits to delivered benefits identifies the gains from technology.

Asking these questions about both existing and new systems can help you identify whether or not technology is or can provide a strategic advantage. There is also the element of risk that must be weighed against the opportunities technology can provide. An example of this can be seen in a new order tracking and delivery initiative under consideration. From initial research it appears to provide opportunities in efficiency and contribute to competitive advantage. When the risks, effects, and probability are evaluated, many are identified. Risks are to current operations, staff retraining, and disruption of customer orders during the changeover. From this analysis two extremely high risks are identified: business disruption and customer retention. If these high risks are mitigated, the new system initiative could be used strategically and provide competitive advantage. One way of identifying risk early is to use the technology assessment described in the next section.

WHAT YOU CAN DO: A TECHNOLOGY ASSESSMENT

Approving new investments is only the beginning. Assessing their capacity to deliver value to corporate objectives and evaluating the results are equally important. Firms that use assessment, measurement, and evaluation techniques realize the highest levels of value from their investments. David Heppenstall of Proctor & Gamble says, "This isn't easy stuff, like office supplies, which are a lot of transactions but not a lot of dollars. These are the big opportunities." He is speaking of the rigor required to assess the opportunities and risks of acquiring new technology against the benefits and value they actually deliver. We have found that the greatest realization of value occurs when up-front research for opportunities and risks is done and reevaluated during and after the investment is implemented. The up-front work identifies the "known unknowns"—risks that can be anticipated because of prior experience with similar technologies. What are often missed are the "unknown unknowns"—the totally unexpected risks that could dramatically disrupt the business. They must be identified as quickly as possible and evaluated for their impact. Managers must then decide whether to mitigate their risks or halt the work. Continuing with technology initiatives when major business risks have been identified ultimately results in missed opportunities and reduced value.

An assessment identifies all technologies that actually exist, how old they are, what they are used for, and what capabilities they have that are not being utilized. An assessment helps to identify technological capability and whether upgrades or new investments are necessary. Before a major investment is undertaken, companies should exploit existing technologies to the fullest. A technology assessment also identifies a company's readiness for technology innovation and documents how the company utilizes technology for vital business programs and processes to deliver customer value. A good assessment shows the current state of technology and its capabilities to support future needs. After this information is gathered, executives can set technology priorities consistent with corporate goals and strategies.

Assessment Steps and Activities for Executive Accountability for Technology

Executives have a key role in both kicking off an assessment and reviewing its results and recommendations. They set the strategic value goals and identify the task force that will be responsible for the assessment. A series of assessment steps drawn from work by Margery Mayer are required to identify needs, prioritize business objectives, and develop strategies for technology investments to deliver value.[6] The outcome of an assessment is a snapshot of current technologies, their use, and their life expectancies. It also provides recommendations for additional technology capabilities that support corporate objectives, priorities, and initiatives. In addition, it provides a roadmap with these priorities and timeframes for upgrading, acquiring, and measuring the benefits and risks of their recommendations. This work leads to business case development for technology redesign or new acquisition to deliver the initiatives and customer benefits.

Step 1: Set the Assessment Goals and Objectives.

Executives determine the purpose, scope, timeframe, budget, and outcomes of the assessment. They also outline how and when action will be taken as a result of the final report and recommendations.

Step 2: Form the Assessment Task Force.

Executives identify the organizational representatives who conduct the assessment. This task force develops the plan for the assessment to meet the goals and objectives.

Step 3: Assess Existing Technology Capabilities.

The task force conducts the actual research required for documenting existing capabilities to deliver business goals and objectives. They work with internal staff to identify business needs and existing technology opportunities.

Step 4: Identify the Needs for New Technology.

The research in the previous steps reveals additional needs that existing technology cannot fill. This step further documents actual business requirements. This documentation identifies what additional functionality is needed and leads to the investigation of new technology.

Step 5: Set Business Priorities for Technology.

Executives now set business priorities for technology to exploit existing systems to their greatest capability. They allocate budget to acquire new technology.

Step 6: Assess Organizational Readiness.

The task force then assesses organizational readiness and staff use of technology and customer attitudes. The assessment documents staff needs and concerns and identifies risks related to business performance and the total customer experience. All implications of technology change on organizational structure, business processes, policies, and management are identified.

Step 7: Set Business Priorities for Process Improvement and Organizational Change.

Executives use input from both assessments and business processes to determine what priorities are needed for organizational structure, policies, and management. Executives have to identify the most critical organizational changes necessary to derive business benefit from the high-priority technology opportunities that support business objectives.

Step 8: Conduct an Opportunity and Risk Evaluation of Technology Plans.

The task force conducts a comprehensive opportunity and risk evaluation to identify the potential benefits as well as the risks that might occur as a result of new technology. These opportunities and risks are then weighed to identify the highest benefit and the most negative effect to better assess the value technology can deliver.

Step 9: Prepare and Present Final Recommendations.

The task force combines all prior information into a findings and recommendations report. This report identifies the current business and technology capabilities and the future needs. It recommends how existing technology can be more fully utilized and new technology acquired to meet business and customer needs. The report also includes the findings and recommendations for organizational readiness and the effect of changes on business performance.

Step 10: Develop Business and Technology Roadmaps.

Roadmaps are developed by executives and are used after the assessment is conducted, findings are developed, and recommendations are delivered. These maps support corporate initiatives and identify where existing and/or new technologies can deliver strategic advantages. Scenarios are developed that exemplify how business and technology can be managed to provide business benefit.

An example of how a technology assessment is applied can be seen in the story of a company whose mission is to be the best at worldwide distribution of consumer products with a goal of growing customer retention by 50 percent. Conducting a technology assessment identifies how technology will be used strategically to support the mission and deliver value. The assessment identifies an existing customer retention level of 25 percent and evaluates whether or not current technology supports the future goal. Current systems allow inquiry access via the Web but does not allow for customer information updates and flexible purchase capability. New technology provides fully integrated systems, high security, and access to real-time payment and delivery processing. The assessment provides additional information regarding potential risks, the impact of new technology on operations, and resource considerations.

Technology investments may be viewed from either an internal or external perspective. For example, an internally focused company looks at whether or not the technology reduces costs or increases productivity of internal operations. Such a company, focused on operations, asks how technology allows for enterprise-wide collaboration for easy access to vital information. A market or externally focused company looks outside at how the technology will change customer perceptions or its position in the market. Such a company looks for ways to enhance customer access to products and services. Organizations that have a market-focused strategy receive the biggest value. Not only do they see value from productivity increases and operations efficiencies, they also receive value from satisfying customer needs and demands. This company achieves returns on investments that provide value and measurable results by supporting the customer experience and increased productivity.

We found that failure to conduct an adequate assessment often leads to underutilized technologies and missed opportunities. A *Computer-World* article[7] states that 70 percent of customer resource management projects fail, even though the technology is considered strategic. If this technology is so strategic, then why have so many companies not achieved the expected strategic value? This article goes on to state that many companies let technology features drive functionality. Instead of applying the assessment rigor for defining the business problem up front and then locating the technology to solve the problem, these companies assume that the technology will address whatever enterprise-wide problems they might have. Such a significant technology change often means modifying business processes and the way staff work. An assessment also identifies roadblocks to achieving value and areas of risk that could disrupt the business. The driver for the investment may not have been its functionality but its potential to deliver business needs and requirements. The decision criteria based on capability to meet business needs drive the selection of technology and investment budget. Lastly, the risks associated with an organization-wide technology solution are identified and strategies developed to minimize risks.

A NEW WAY OF THINKING: EXECUTIVE ACCOUNTABILITY FOR TECHNOLOGY VALUE

We believe a new way of thinking is necessary to deliver strategic value from technology. Managers at all levels must understand and use technology as an asset and as an integral, essential component in delivering products and services to meet market demands. They need to be able to correctly assess the current and future business needs to evaluate alternative technology options. Technology decisions and acquisitions should be designed to result in a contribution to business value and long-term performance. All executives and managers have clear accountability for obtaining these benefits and value from technology. Managers need to know how to work collaboratively when applying technology solutions that integrate their different skills, how to resolve concerns, and how to identify business needs. Lastly, managers must assess the risks to the business from technology investments and continually evaluate actual business outcomes.

What You Can Do: Hold a Technology Summit

We use the idea of a technology summit to illustrate how a new way of thinking about technology is an organization-wide responsibility. Following is a technology summit scenario.

The chief executive officer recognizes the importance of including technology in the corporate strategic planning process and is committed to obtaining the best knowledge about technology and its use across the organization. One of the senior executives sponsors a "technology summit" to prepare for the annual business-planning event. Executives and managers research, collaborate, and recommend answers to questions about how technology will strengthen overall business performance and growth. The questions to be answered are:

- How do we adopt and adapt technology as an essential foundation to the operating life and future of the business?

- How can we continue to improve our organization-wide strategic decisions about technology to ensure that they benefit the business?

- How do we meet the technology requirements of autonomous profit centers?

- What changes to our culture and competencies do we need to make to utilize technology for competitive advantage?

- How do we structure accountability and incentives among executives and business and technology managers for realizing results from technology investments?

Executives and managers have the results of a recent technology assessment to help them prepare for the summit. The assessment identifies the research and analysis necessary to make specific recommendations on technology strategy. Managers come prepared to address staff needs and concerns about technology. All managers bring proposals to address organizational change issues.

During the summit, all divisions and business units are represented and share their findings and recommendations. The business unit representatives first present technology opportunities for their function or line of business. They also present possible benefits the entire company can obtain by integrating different technologies and improving the infrastructure to achieve strategic objectives. Each unit also identifies the opportunities and risks of investing in technology. Debate and discussion of what is best for the company and its units is strongly encouraged.

At the conclusion of this summit, all participants understand what the high priorities are for company infrastructure and unit-level technology systems. Accountability for preparing the organization and improving technology to support business strategy is clearly identified. When the executive team begins the strategic business planning effort they have the best recommendations with analysis and evaluation from the entire organization.

Following the business planning effort, the executive team and staff prioritize and update business performance objectives and evaluation processes for technology investments. Measurement of business benefits from technology are linked to rewards and recognition. Executives are confident that measurable business opportunities and benefits have not been overlooked or unrealistically overestimated. There is defined executive oversight and an initiative review process that encompasses launch, implementation, and utilization.

WHAT YOU CAN DO: IMPLEMENT ORGANIZATION-WIDE ACCOUNTABILITY

Executives, middle management, technologists, and business staff are all accountable for working together constructively to produce benefits for customers and the business. Using the assessment, the company can develop organization-wide accountabilities for realizing the value from technology. IT is responsible for how technology can provide the capability to meet business needs. Business units are accountable for improving business processes to meet market and customer demands. All other functional roles and accountabilities should be specified for technology initiatives. Everyone is accountable for effective collaboration.

How does this organization-wide approach to business benefits from technology differ from the current approach? In the current approach, technology implementation is often delegated to middle management and IT staff, with executive involvement primarily for funding and project approval. The new strategic approach to technology investments depends on an accountability structure that starts at the executive level. There is an ongoing and timely executive oversight process so that initiatives progress efficiently, and troubled projects are adjusted quickly or cancelled.

This new thinking may seem like a dream—an unachievable goal—but the dream of a better way to strategically manage technology for benefits is achievable. Figure 3.2 illustrates how all parts of the internal organization interact with external parties for benefit of customers and organization growth. We have observed our clients complete technology projects where accountability and commitment is understood at all levels to produce clear and measurable results. Customers write letters to management and call to praise exciting new products and services. These experiences are exhilarating. Staff gain tremendous satisfaction by making an important contribution to business value. Executives also realize that they can rely on staff to deliver actual results linked to important business goals.

Figure 3.2
Organization-Wide Accountability for Value

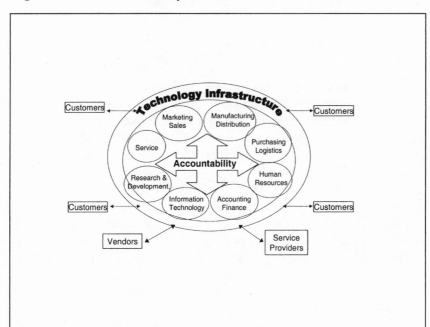

Achieving This New Way of Thinking

A metaphor can illustrate how an organization thinks and acts strategically about technology. A strategic thinking approach to technology is like dropping a rock into a pond and following the pattern of waves across the pond and onto the shore. The pond is actually a combination of the existing technology infrastructure and all business activity. Interaction between the business and the technology infrastructure is what customers, investors, and other external parties use to form perceptions of the business and its organizational performance and success.

When the rock of new or modified technology drops into the pond of the technology infrastructure and operating environment, waves are created that merge with existing patterns and affect worker productivity, managerial effectiveness, and customer perceptions. Executives and managers are able to introduce new technology rocks into vital markets and not be surprised by unexpected waves that cross the pond and hit the shores. Staff are well prepared to utilize technology immediately and customers are never aware of technology changes. Executives now know the short- and long-term effects of new technology (the ripples on the shore) on the total infrastructure, operating environment, and business performance.

SUMMARY

Realizing the strategic value from technology is realizing the benefits and enhanced performance it can deliver. If technology strategy is integrated into executive thinking when planning corporate direction, goals, and objectives, its advantages are more likely to be identified and achieved. Executive ownership is critical in helping the whole organization understand how value, benefits, and results are attained from technology. Lack of input from executives could result in a missed opportunity to increase the value of the company and utilize all resources effectively. The executive who utilizes technology strategically gives the company a competitive edge and misses no opportunity to do this. It is not enough to implicitly support technology investments and then question the disappointing results. If executives really want to realize the strategic value from technology, they need to understand its capabilities and effects on company value.

QUESTIONS FOR REFLECTION AND DISCUSSION

1. How do you know if a technology provides for future needs?
2. How do you know if the technology that has been acquired in the past has delivered strategic value?
3. How can you ensure that future acquisitions of technology will deliver value?
4. How do you conduct technology assessments?
5. How do you conduct organizational readiness assessments?
6. How do you develop a strategic IT plan?
7. What measures do you have in place to prove that your technology investments provide a strategic advantage?

NOTES

1. "Building IT Infrastructure for the 1990's," *ComputerWorld* (June 8, 1992): 93–94, referenced work by D. T. McKay, and D. W. Brockway, *Stage by Stage*. New York: Nolan Norton KPMG, 1989.

2. Davenport, T. "The New, New IT Strategy." *CIO Magazine* (May 1, 2001), from CIO website archives at www.cio.com.

3. FedEx, Web site www.fedex.com/us/about/overview/technology/link = 4, November 2002.

4. Sabre, Web site www.com/about/index2html?b + history/index.html, November 2002.

5. Limited Brands, Web site www.limitedbrands.com/whoweare/, November 2002.

6. Mayer, M., "Technology Assessment Papers" for Client Consulting, 1997.

7. Dunne, D. "Beware of CRM Backlash," *ComputerWorld* (February 6, 2002): 1–10.

Part II

SHIFTING TO ORGANIZATION-WIDE THINKING ABOUT BUSINESS BENEFITS

Chapter 4

BUILDING ORGANIZATION-WIDE PROCESSES FOR DELIVERING VALUE FROM TECHNOLOGY

When we asked the project director whose story opened Chapter 2, Understanding the Victim's View of Technology, what he needed to be more successful, he said a holistic approach to management of his large project. By "holistic" he meant an approach in which accountability for benefits from technology investments is organization-wide. Based on experience in multimillion dollar technology initiatives over two to three years, we have found that initiatives are successful only when accountability at every level, in every part of the company, and with all partners is defined at the outset and maintained throughout the life of the implementation.

In the late 1990s, the requirements to meet Y2K deadlines caused a shift from technology being implemented by function or business process to implementation by organization-wide initiatives that often included upgrading the entire infrastructure. Executives made the decisions that funded initiatives and launched projects. Oversight and organization-wide accountabilities were then delegated to IT and to middle managers to define, staff, and operate. Y2K initiatives were defined from a narrow technical perspective, even though their effects could directly and indirectly touch many areas of the business. In these implementations, staff stayed within the scope of the technical project and did not consider all of the work that needed to be done for customers and the organization to derive the greatest benefit. An assumption was made that repercussions across the organization after projects were completed could be easily corrected with some additional overtime by staff.

Political battles—positioning for control of the project and system features—create confusion that cannot be resolved through status meetings and project procedures. To eliminate misdirected energy and resources, which include policies, processes, operational planning, and executive oversight, companies need an ongoing organizational structure for technology. To avoid the problems encountered during initiative efforts, organization structure must be focused on the benefits and business value to be gained from technology. Organization structure must support the success of tactical technology and business projects that are linked to broader business objectives. By clarifying and establishing organization-wide goals for technology initiatives, a decision process, collaboration, and action plans, executives and staff can effectively move technology initiatives ahead and in some cases more than exceed their goals.

Executive accountability for investments in technology is critical if the investments are to meet market demands, create customer value, and strengthen the financial position of their organization. However, executives are not often provided with practical, tested, models or tools to assist them in making their organizations successful. A clear business plan that connects the strategic direction of the organization to investments in and use of technology is necessary. An accountable executive provides ongoing direction and asks thought-provoking questions across the enterprise to ensure that technology initiatives meet customer needs.

This chapter gives examples of executive accountability through four management approaches that reduce the victim experience while solving real business problems. We outline the strengths and constraints associated with executive approaches that, in our experience, are the most prevalent and that have most dramatically influenced positive business results. The four management approaches identified are delegation, crisis/reactive, strong involvement, and visionary. Each approach significantly affects the outcome of a technology investment. Later in the chapter we reinforce the importance of strategic thinking for technology investments. We conclude with a model that outlines strategic, organization-wide, and local accountability. Using this model allows organizations to shift from short-term budget and priority battles for technology investments to a greater focus on business benefits for long-term sustainability and company performance.

EXECUTIVE APPROACHES TO MAXIMIZE BENEFITS AND RESULTS FROM TECHNOLOGY INVESTMENTS

Executives are more involved in large or high-risk technology initiatives when expected benefits are not delivered or because the success of the initiative is critical to the company's future. Combinations of executive approaches exist within the same company and any approach could be successful, depending on the situation. Different risks are associated with each of the executive approaches. It is important that an executive is aware of the risks of his or her approach in order to minimize those risks. In our discussion of each executive approach, we identify the level of involvement necessary to address the urgency or risk for achieving a business benefit without constraining management or staff productivity. When an approach is used successfully, it should be recognized and repeated in similar situations. Review your approach to managing technology over the entire course of initiatives and compare it to the following executive approaches. This comparison will assist you in identifying successful ways of managing technology for company benefit.

Executive Approach 1: Delegation

The executive role in this approach is to approve the budget and ensure that proposals are consistent with strategic goals. Middle managers develop the proposals, make the technology decisions, create the plans, formulate budget requests, and lead the implementation. Executives expect middle management to deliver the technology to meet the business need and customer requirements. If middle management is highly effective at combining technology strategy with proposal development and implementation, this hands-off approach can work effectively.

We have observed the success of the delegation approach in a successful $5 million enterprise software project that met 100 percent of the desired results. In this project, the investigation of an enterprise-wide software solution was delegated to middle management in a division of a company with approximately $100 million in yearly revenue. A year in advance, key business managers and the IT department identified needs and investigated a solution. The business strategy, requirements, decision criteria, and key business process changes were determined early and used to guide the software product selection. When the software was selected, an experienced project manager was hired to lead the implementation. He insisted that business management and the technology project team take joint ownership of the system implementation. Consultants with product experience were brought in to transfer system knowledge to the internal business staff. The software was integrated in accordance with business needs and the technical staff confirmed that the requirements were met. Business processes were mapped and analyzed, training for end users was developed, and regular communication meetings were conducted. A primary challenge for the project was to reduce the effect of increased volume of data entry in order-entry tasks for the operations. Initially the project team had incorrectly estimated the magnitude of the change for all staff involved in the process. The project team was later able to eliminate this issue by assisting the operation's staff to adapt to the system. They were able to eliminate all critical issues within 60 days after the system was completed.

Factors That Made the Delegation Approach Successful

- Executives allowed for extensive analysis of business needs, processes, and product vendors.
- Executives were well informed and were confident of the approved business objectives, project scope, budget, and implementation plans.
- Knowledgeable management staff researched the business processes, improvements, and product selection criteria.
- The project manager developed the business team members' competency in implementing the selected technology product.
- Management adjusted time and resource allocations to deliver the desired business results.
- The project was designed for joint ownership by technology experts and business management over the entire work effort.
- Managers had ready access to executives to quickly resolve business-operating issues within short time frames.
- Staff were highly experienced and had an interest in learning about business technology and project management.
- The executive was proactive in seeking technology solutions and obtaining funding to support his divisional business needs.

Potential Risks of the Delegation Approach

A primary risk for the delegation approach is inadequate competency of staff in project management, technology evaluation, and knowledge of the business.

Delegation does not work well if staff have not been in their positions very long and have only a general understanding of how the business operates. The challenges with technology are in the details, and staff must be able to identify risks of changes in data, processing rules, and interconnections with other systems and organizations. When managers are using technology only for tactical improvements, large investments may be made that only automate existing and inefficient processes and procedures. An ancillary opportunity cost is that staff focused only on tactical benefits for a specific functional need may never seek out broader benefits for the business and related functions. In addition, tactical managers are unlikely to identify and escalate strategic issues that have to be resolved at the executive level.

Another risk of delegation is that the executive could disregard data compiled by staff and make decisions based on criteria hidden from the team. In this situation, staff may become demoralized because their best efforts are disregarded. If the executive believes it is necessary to make a top-down decision with only input from staff, he or she must communicate this at the outset of the initiative.

Executive Approach 2: Crisis/Reactive

In this approach, the executive acts only when there is a sudden external demand or internal crisis. Events that might spark crisis/reactive management are failures of critical systems, insufficient capacity, increase of transaction volume on existing systems, competition, mergers and acquisitions, and sudden economic or market changes. An example of the success of the crisis/reactive management approach is demonstrated by an initiative to replace a payment processing system that failed in a major global bank division. This critical system consolidated and edited customer transactions from all over the world via 13 different interfacing systems. When thousands of dollars of customer transactions were temporarily lost and were difficult to recover, the executive created an emergency task force to build a total replacement system. This task force was given a preliminary budget and target completion date. The task force was encouraged to use the methodology of its choice and given the most knowledgeable resources to define, launch, and implement new technology. Corporate standards for full system replacements were very stringent and ensured that financial balancing and control routines were accurate and would protect customer accounts. The replacement system was installed smoothly and accurately over three years. A process for executive oversight with quarterly reviews was used to manage changes to the budget, scope, and schedule. Accounting management and staff were involved in the initiative from the beginning and developed a system requirements "Bible" that guided the refinement and operational implementation as well as technology development. The completed system improved financial controls, streamlined reporting, and met the documented business requirements.

Factors That Made the Crisis/Reactive Approach Successful

- In crisis, the executive acted quickly to approve and fund an initiative to replace the aging system.
- Staff skilled in project management and business needs analysis were allocated to identify requirements, project scope, budget, and process improvement recommendations.
- The executive adjusted the budget and schedule to ensure that the project was successful and met business needs.
- The executive created and led the project review process for rapid issue resolution, schedule changes, and budget control.
- Corporate staff from accounting and bank reconciliation worked closely with divisional staff to ensure that the system met all regulatory requirements and company standards

Potential Risks of the Crisis/Reactive Approach

If the executive is using a crisis/reactive approach to technology investments, waiting for a crisis to trigger actions and decisions often causes the "too little, too late" syndrome. Too often the time for analysis and research of alternatives is cut short when technology reaches a crisis condition. Product selection and vendors may not be thoroughly researched, and purchase decisions are often made hastily. Technology projects launched in a crisis may result in the selection of inappropriate products and implementation of short-term solutions that often have to be replaced to meet increased business needs. They may also be subject to runaway budgets or uncontrolled spending, if the executive creates a climate of "fix the system at all costs." Of greater impact to the long-term success of the company is that waiting for crises opens the door for competitors to take market share and valued customers. Under the crisis climate, IT staff do not have an opportunity to research the technology used by competitors and develop longer-term technology strategies for the company. A short-term fix could negatively affect product and service development plans that could in turn affect valuable revenue streams. Quick-fix technology might have to be replaced in a short time, thereby increasing costs.

Executive Approach 3: Strong Involvement

In this situation a strong executive is responsible for major decisions and accepts ownership for the results. An example of this approach is an executive director of a state department of employment, who took personal accountability for measurable business results from technology investments. The agency had an initiative to develop an online program that would allow applicants to find and match their skills to available jobs. This initiative would rocket the state into an electronic, Internet-based mode where it could provide services for local businesses with open positions as well as job seekers. The goal was to gain corporate sponsorship for a one-stop online system that would provide significant benefits. Millions of dollars were allocated for this significant and much-publicized initiative.

The technical task force did research into what other states had already developed in this area to learn from others instead of creating technology from scratch. Analysis revealed that two states had systems that met similar needs to theirs. The task force conducted site visits to view these systems and developed a cost/benefit analysis to acquire and customize either of these systems. They found that cost and time savings from acquiring and modifying another state's system were impressive. The task force presented the findings to the executive director and received legislative approval. The executive director was involved in the negotiations and even visited the other state to see for himself how the system was being used. Upon his return, the he reviewed all the documentation and approved the team direction. He participated in the user testing to better understand how the final system would feel for customers. His positive involvement was critical to the task force and to the overall success of the initiative. Although he was deeply involved in critical decision making, he did not attempt to micromanage or take over, but he gave the task force the support it needed to complete a very public initiative to meet legislative and customer expectations.

Factors That Made the Strong Involvement Approach Successful

- There was accountability for this effort at the executive director, advisory council, and legislature levels.

- The executive had a compelling vision and the advisory council defined clear business requirements.

- A very qualified task force from software development, technology systems, financial analysis, and project management was created. It thoroughly researched technology opportunities.

- A cost/benefit analysis was conducted that identified cost and time saving benefits.
- The executive supported the task force and was involved in the negotiations.
- All related agencies were provided with guidelines on how to share in the benefits of the initiative.

Potential Risks of the Strong Involvement Approach

The strongly involved executive can cause a bottleneck in direction setting and decision making. Such a bottleneck can impede rapid adjustments to meet customer demands. Some strong executives insist on making decisions even at the lowest level of detail. If a process is not in place to escalate appropriate decisions quickly, the implementation team can be stalled, waiting for direction. There is an important distinction between a strong and involved executive and one who exerts such high control over the initiative that staff morale deteriorates, quality of work suffers, and commitment to the success of the project is stifled. If the executive is unsure of management's capabilities to analyze and make good decisions, then a pattern of second guessing recommendations occurs. This approach can confuse accountability and cause initiatives to stagnate.

Executive Approach 4: Visionary

This approach involves a strong visionary leader who understands the value of strategic planning and invests in technology to generate long-term business growth. She includes key executives and managers in the strategic planning and decision-making processes. This executive acknowledges the expertise that others bring and creates opportunities for people across the organization to use technology as a strategic asset.

An example of this approach is an executive director who was appointed to turn around a failing city transportation system because the community was clamoring for more efficiency. He had a vision for improving both the operating performance of the organization and the public's perception of service quality.

When he arrived, a project was already underway to replace the existing technology that controlled the light rail system with new technology that was more sophisticated than other transportation control systems. The project had been estimated to take four years and cost about $80 million. It was already three years behind schedule and running about $10 million over budget when he took over. In addition, only 35 percent of the work had been completed.

He found that the project was delayed because the software did not have the full functionality promised by the vendor. The prior project manager allowed frequent changes to the functional requirements and did not have a project change management process in place. The executive director realized that the project was out of control and needed an experienced software project manager. He hired a consultant who stated that the entire contract had to be renegotiated before work could proceed. The consultant recommended that specific deliverables and milestones be identified and documented and that the contract allow no changes or additions to the requirements. With a clearer contract in place the project proceeded.

During the final testing of the software and railway system, a decision had to be made about whether to shut down service to test the systems during peak periods or to test only during off hours. The executive director made the decision to test off hours and put the system into service after partial testing. He did not believe the riders would accept a slow-down or cancellation of regular commute service for further testing. He realized this decision could have negative consequences and understood the risks.

The system went live on a Monday morning and had problems for the entire first week. The trains broke down in peak commute times and some commuters were hours late. The press publicized the breakdowns and customer dissatisfaction, which intensified the public perception of another failure in service. The executive director relied on his software consultant to fix the problems, and a week later the transportation system was meeting expected levels of service. This executive took full accountability for his decisions and met with the press and the public on a daily basis until the problems were corrected. Today the train system runs smoothly and public approval of the transportation system has improved.

Factors That Made the Visionary Approach Successful

- The executive director had a strategic view for how technology would meet organizational and public needs.
- The strategic needs of the organization guided his decisions.
- A knowledgeable professional in software development and project management identified the key problems and addressed them immediately.
- The executive took accountability for the project even under severe pressure.

Potential Risks of the Visionary Approach

The visionary executive must secure strong support from his or her board of directors, investors, and internal staff to be successful. Executives can be so caught up in the vision that their ability to translate the vision for staff who are implementing it is limited. The executive must also have the capability to obtain the funding and appropriate resources to implement the vision. Without adequate resources, implementation of the vision can be cut short. Another risk is that the vision might be based on an incorrect understanding of the market and customers. The executive's vision needs to be validated by customer, market, or organizational need, or the company's survival could be at risk.

The key concept from the discussion of these management approaches is that executive accountability is required for the success of technology initiatives. Executives set the tone and pattern for the entire organization's accountability for delivering benefits from technology. If any of these executives walked away from the situation and staff were confused about their accountability, benefits from technology would never be realized. Their accountability and their commitment to the success of their technology initiatives gave their entire organization the focus and drive to deliver benefits.

MODEL: ORGANIZATION-WIDE ACCOUNTABILITY FOR VALUE FROM TECHNOLOGY

Our organization-wide model for value from technology accountability is the result of a shift from thinking about individual products and tools to thinking strategically about an infrastructure and business management environment that delivers benefits to customers. This model provides a framework of accountability at all levels of the organization and across all profit and cost centers, functions, and professional specialties to secure customer satisfaction, operational efficiencies, and long-term growth. The model allows for frustrations and issues with technology to be voiced in a way that supports value for customers and business. It also highlights the increasing importance of organization-wide collaboration and decision making for technology reaching across the entire enterprise and positively affecting the overall business performance.

This model is based on the need to meet customers' needs. The company uses technology strategically to communicate with customers and motivate them to acquire its products and services. Customers can con-

Figure 4.1
Organization-Wide Accountability for Value from Technology

veniently update account data or contact service from their homes, at work, or in transit. For this reason, the technology infrastructure in this model is represented by an oval that reaches beyond the physical boundaries of the company. It allows customers many access routes to information. The company must know the patterns of customer interaction and satisfaction, gather this information, and analyze the information to find opportunities to generate revenue or reduce expenses. The overall quality of the customer experience is managed to secure loyalty and repeat business.

The inner oval in this model represents the physical company. Staff use technology to perform their daily work, find better ways to operate the business, and satisfy customers. The model clearly illustrates that information must be shared to identify business opportunities, reduce risks, and ensure customer value. Staff accountability means ensuring that the right technology is selected and implemented to meet business needs. Managers are accountable for ensuring that the technology is accurately and effectively used to preserve the quality of information and support customer needs.

Three Levels of Accountability

The model has three levels of accountability for deriving business value from technology investments: strategic, organization-wide, and local. The first level, strategic accountability, means executives are responsible for creating the business environment where increasing business value is the goal of investing in technology. Executives set the strategic direction, business objectives, and organizational structure necessary for deriving benefits from technology. This is usually done through a formal strategic plan, annual business plan, and definition of objectives for the company. Strategic accountability also includes setting policies, processes, performance targets, and measures for how technology initiatives are formed, managed, and evaluated. A critical element of strategic accountability is the effective executive oversight process for all technology investments. This oversight process ensures that initiatives are linked to business objectives and that executives are aware of any important opportunities, risks, or changes that affect achieving business benefits. Even though executives delegate the technology implementation work to managers and staff, they are ultimately accountable for the reliability of company information, how it is used, and its effect on business performance.

The second level, organization-wide accountability, represents middle management's role for collaboration and decisions necessary for enterprise-wide benefits to be realized. In the model, parallel activities among the IT and business functions must be rigorously integrated to support business benefits from initiatives. Managers and staff from profit centers, cost centers, functions, and external suppliers all have to share their specialized expertise and jointly develop business cases, requirements, and plans. In addition, they evaluate the readiness of the organization for products and services and plan how the technology will be phased into the existing infrastructure and business processes. Middle managers apply decision-making processes and tools, communicate, and collaborate over the entire course of the initiatives. Negotiations of tough trade-offs among technology and business line interests are necessary to deliver organization-wide business benefits from technology.

The third level is local accountability, in which each function or business line is accountable for technology initiatives within its span of control and has little effect on the organization as a whole. These systems are used to accomplish tasks unique to that function and are often not integrated with enterprise systems. Examples of local accountability are spreadsheet analysis and other tasks done on desktop systems used by that business line only. This local level is also accountable for identifying when local systems would provide greater benefit to the organization if integrated into the enterprise.

The benefit of our model is that organizations can use it to look beyond their boundaries for bigger, more strategic business benefits. For example, it may be appropriate for finance to lead an initiative to improve accounts payable management. The sponsor and task force identify the business needs and work closely with the technology specialists. They realize that an important step is to negotiate with profit and cost centers to identify organization-wide changes and benefits. Any department can voice concerns that affect the company and can negotiate for time to improve better business readiness into the plans for the new system. The technology is then implemented for specific units of the company. Departments requesting later adaptation may come online at a later time.

The Four Management Approaches and the Accountability Model

All of the management approaches for technology can increase benefits from technology. In the delegation approach, the executive uses the model to ensure that business knowledge is shared and collaboration is encouraged to identify and validate business benefits from technology. The executive designs the oversight process to ensure that strategic issues are identified, that such issues are escalated to the right level of management, and that only critical strategic issues reach the highest-level decisionmaker. In the crisis/reactive approach, the executive uses the model to rapidly identify gaps in accountability that add risk to technology initiatives. Clear accountability for all staff assigned to the crisis initiative means that staff know where to go to rapidly resolve issues and make adjustments. In the strong executive approach, lines of control and decision making are clearly defined at all levels in the organization and linked to the executive. Bottlenecks in communication and decisions are reduced if everyone knows how and when to obtain access to the executive. For the visionary approach, the model provides a map for executives to build communication plans to translate the vision into commitment and action across the organization. This clear communication allows staff to take the vision and translate it into tangible technology investments that deliver value to the company.

The Organization-Wide Accountability Model and Generation of Business Value

This model supports the generation of business value and ensures that all parts of the organization are appropriately involved in technology initiatives at the right time. With this organization-wide view, hidden costs of implementation are revealed and managed; benefits to customers and internal staff are identified, more accurately estimated, and validated; and important improvements in business operations as a whole are discovered.

WHAT YOU CAN DO: APPLY THE ORGANIZATION-WIDE ACCOUNTABILITY MODEL TO TECHNOLOGY INITIATIVES

1. In the research and initiation stage of initiatives, build an organization-wide process for collaboration. In these early stages it is important to get the knowledge and views of those who are accountable for implementing and delivering value when the initiative is completed. By engaging key individuals at each level of accountability, the reliability of the analysis and estimates of business benefits is increased.

2. During the implementation stages, establish a decision-making structure that includes all levels of accountability. This is a critical step in co-ordinating multiple projects that support a single initiative. Decisions can then be made within the appropriate scope of authority to keep the project on track.

3. After initiative completion, measure and evaluate the results. Communicate the key outcomes of the initiative to the organization.

4. Use lessons learned from the prior actions to increase the business benefits from future initiatives.

SUMMARY

We identify four prevalent approaches to accountability—delegation, crisis/reactive, strong involvement, and visionary—each with its strengths and risks. There are other approaches as well, and organizations should use whatever works to deliver value from technology investments.

Organization-wide accountability is essential and such accountability must be clear for technology initiatives to deliver value. Knowing that the appropriate level of the organization is accountable for the different success criteria of technology initiatives is critical. Executives' accountability is for strategic and organizational oversight and decision making.

Organization-wide accountability includes the negotiations, collaboration, and decisions that affect broad areas of the business such as profit centers, divisions, or the entire organization. It is important that these managers share their knowledge, redesign business processes, and make collaborative decisions. Local accountability is applied to functional and departmental projects to achieve specific benefits. It is important to consider whether local needs are consistent with company objectives. We encourage executives to use this model to increase accountability for ensuring that the business value derived from technology provides a long-term benefit.

QUESTIONS FOR REFLECTION AND DISCUSSION

1. How is accountability for business results from technology investments defined in your company?

2. What management approaches are used in your company, and how effective are they in delivering value from technology investments?

3. How do you address the risks each approach brings and still deliver technology for business value?

4. How do you know if new technology has a positive or negative effect on customer behavior?

5. How is accountability managed at each level of the organization?

6. How effectively is accountability outlined and managed for technology investments that reach across many business lines, functions, and regions?

Chapter 5

CREATING A STRUCTURE FOR ORGANIZATION-WIDE COLLABORATION

At its best, effective collaboration is a creative process that translates the long-term vision and strategies of the company into clear objectives and initiatives. Effective collaboration within organizations is critical for deriving benefits from technology investments. At the outset of initiatives, collaboration generates compelling ideas through analysis and weighing risks against opportunities. Collaboration is also important to establishing organization-wide accountability for business results from technology and commitment to action and completion. Implementation of technology initiatives requires managers, staff, technologists, vendors, and other support groups to work together intensively for extended periods of time. Exploration and debate of issues reduces risks in business analysis, improves estimation of benefits, and increases the accuracy and completeness of implementation plans. Information from external and internal sources must also be shared, analyzed, and evaluated to deliver value and benefits to customers and the company.

However, collaboration is not easy to establish and maintain for long periods of time. It is inherently temporary and frequently cannot be transferred from one group to another. For effective collaboration to last over the entire course of technology initiatives, it must be an important activity for executives, managers, and staff. It is more sustainable when it is structured and meets a specific business purpose, applies principles for interaction, defines staff capabilities, and is conducted with supporting methods and tools. Effective collaboration does not depend on outgoing personalities and friendly people. It requires individuals who are committed to leveraging all viewpoints, working through challenging discussions and disagreements to arrive at bursts of creativity and well-thought-out ideas and actions. The larger the technology initiative, the more its success depends on a structured and formal collaboration process that is fine-tuned to the organization management approach.

In this chapter we provide a framework for building organization-wide collaboration that has assisted companies in achieving greater business results for large or critical technology initiatives. We will describe alternatives for developing collaboration to overcome barriers caused by organizational reporting lines and subcultures. Variations for collaboration structure are linked to the different management approaches for technology. This examination highlights the vital role executives play in building the bridges across the organization to support collaboration. A number of methods and tools are provided, such as including collaboration in the business readiness assessment, planning working sessions with trained meeting facilitators, and mapping a path for collaboration.

AN ORGANIZATION-WIDE FRAMEWORK FOR COLLABORATION

Organization-wide collaboration must reach across all levels, units, functions, regions, and professional specialties. Collaboration can also be formal or informal. An example of formal collaboration is a monthly or quarterly review wherein managers report on periodic business performance and operating effectiveness. In this review, budgets, progress toward completion, and high priority issues are identified and resolved. Examples of informal collaboration are ad hoc meetings or hallway conversations where staff discuss issues, accomplish tasks, and advance technology initiatives. Informal collaboration is a way to socialize ideas, gather support, and test controversial topics. It sets the groundwork for important decisions that are often made in more formal collaboration settings. When decisions must be made for organization-wide technology systems, extensive collaboration is required before goals, plans, and actions can be considered complete.

Figure 5.1 illustrates three directions in which collaboration takes place in organizations: vertical, horizontal, and bottom-up. All three forms of collaboration are essential for organizations to be more informed and productive as technology initiatives become more complex.

Figure 5.1
Organization-Wide Collaboration

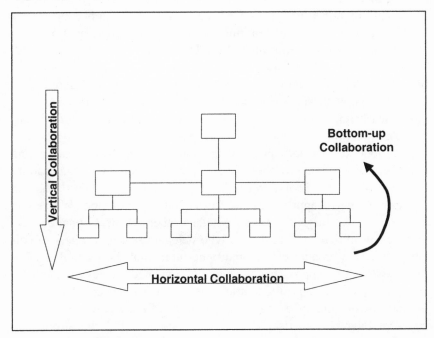

Vertical Collaboration

Vertical collaboration is sometimes referred to as top-down communication. In this type of collaboration, executives solicit formal and informal recommendations and views from senior managers and staff. Vertical collaboration may be used to clarify, refine, and implement objectives and initiatives. After taking this input and approving resulting objectives, directives and assignments are communicated down into the organization. When vertical collaboration is effective, the managers who execute the objectives are more committed to achieving them. This is the most common management approach.

Horizontal Collaboration

This important activity supports organization-wide accountability by sharing information and ideas from different managers, functions, and specialties for a specific business purpose. Horizontal collaboration frequently is an ongoing, informal daily activity. It may occur in small group meetings and task forces where a constant flow of e-mail supports collaboration. Typically, status meetings and issue resolution meetings occur to track the detailed progress of the initiative. Formal decision-making meetings with management decision makers occur when budget, scope, and high-priority issues must be addressed. Examples are cross-functional task forces collaborating horizontally on implementing technology initiatives with specialists from IT, consultants, and internal staff from finance, quality assurance, or legal services. Horizontal collaboration also includes bringing distributed staff together from different geographic regions to support product lines and functions. For example, global marketing managers collaborate to identify different country market conditions for the same product or service.

Let's look at how horizontal collaboration can vary widely depending on the management approaches from chapter four, Building Organization-Wide Processes for Delivering Value from Technology. The delegation and crisis/reactive approaches use horizontal collaboration. With these approaches, executive determine whether other business functions are involved in initiatives. Executives who delegate seek out others to collaborate on the broader effects and opportunities of the technology. For the crisis/reactive approach, the technology change creates a crisis situation in which there is often little time for horizontal collaboration in the interest of quickly fixing the problem. The crisis/reactive approach can actually raise the risks for the new solution. For the strong and visionary management approaches, it is again up to the discretion of top executives as to how horizontal collaboration is used. A strong executive may use horizontal collaboration to support the initiative by identifying broad opportunities and risks. A visionary executive encourages collaboration to gather support for initiatives and information that will lead to its success.

Bottom-up Collaboration

This type of collaboration is characterized by middle management or staff identifying and proposing technology ideas or communicating issues and concerns about the risks of initiatives. This collaboration is important because issues they identify can affect business performance. Incorrect data or processing can prevent products from reaching customers and cause major business disruptions. In the delegation and crisis/reactive approaches there is a critical need for accurate, complete, and timely bottom-up collaboration and communication to support the initiatives. The strong and visionary management approaches make discretionary decisions on how much bottom-up collaboration to use. Bottom-up collaboration must be supported by a formal structure for these management approaches. In our experience, often bottom-up collaboration is a new concept to executives and managers. Because of this, staff may be hesitant to provide bottom-up feedback and information unless the guidelines for doing so are approved and encouraged by the executive. However, when this form of collaboration is working effectively, the organization can deliver technology initiatives more rapidly, with lower risk and greater value.

HOW TO KNOW WHEN COLLABORATION IS EFFECTIVE

Executives know when collaboration is effective because they can enjoy its results. Effective collaboration produces clear objective statements for technology with well-coordinated plans and measurable results. Executives see proposals for global product development, external alliances, and internal productivity or customer satisfaction from various perspectives through collaboration efforts. How collaboration is used can be documented. Documentation should include a clear business purpose and guiding principles that lead to cooperative action. Staff can then efficiently use the recommended processes, methods, and tools to support collaboration. When collaboration is effective, evaluation and feedback to improve it is ongoing.

When issues are escalated to executives, clear alternatives reflecting different perspectives should be proposed to resolve them. There is less opinion, more research, and more evaluation of information across the organization. Dissenting views are encouraged and articulated early in initiative formation to improve the quality of the specific objectives and implementation plans. With this rich support from collaboration, executives are more able to enhance the quality of their decision making and the value of technology to the organization.

Examples of effective collaboration are frequently observable during the discovery of new pharmaceuticals. Researchers share expertise and collaborate through on-line methods.[1] Communities of practice methods using electronic tools for collaboration bring together managers and staff with similar industry knowledge, education, and professional experiences.[2] Schrage suggests that time to market is reduced and the value of new products and services is increased when development teams collaborate using prototypes, models, and simulations to meet customer needs.

Collaboration is ineffective when staff attend long meetings discussing the technology with little tangible output. They leave without a shared statement of the key business objectives, course of action, or issue resolution. When staff are asked about the purpose and guiding principles for collaboration, the answers vary widely. In addition, methods and tools for collaboration may not exist or be widely known and used. This gap, unknown to executives, allows them to assume that the funded initiatives are progressing until a crisis occurs relating to technology. This high-risk situation affects daily operations and raises important questions about why the risks of the technology were not communicated or esca-lated earlier. When initiatives and their related projects are in trouble, the cause may be that vertical, horizontal, or bottom-up collaboration did not occur. It is very important that collaboration occurs when organiza-tion-wide efforts are underway because their success depends on it. Table 5.1 contrasts effective collaboration and ineffective collaboration.

HOW TO STRUCTURE COLLABORATION

Define the Purpose of Collaboration for Each Initiative

For collaboration to produce a result, it needs to happen in the context of a clear business purpose that is linked to business objectives and

Table 5.1
Effective and Ineffective Collaboration

Effective Collaboration	Ineffective Collaboration
Clear business purpose for collaboration stated	Efforts of individuals can be redundant or misdirected
Guiding principles stated	Team members are working at cross purposes
Processes, methods, and tools for collaboration defined and used	Recreating processes, methods, and tools for collaboration instead of completing tasks
Evaluation and feedback among individuals and groups occur frequently	Individuals and groups have no idea if they are delivering value
Recommendations may include different perspectives of an issue and/or dissenting views	Individuals are afraid to express dissenting views, increasing risks
Escalation path to upper management is defined	Failure to escalate increases risks

individual performance. General appeals to increase collaboration across organizations do not lead to important business results and are often meaningless. Staff must be convinced that collaboration is essential to reduce the risk and achieve the benefits of initiatives. The business purpose must be compelling enough to make staff collaborate automatically, even if they have not worked together before.

Here is an example of how executives required results from research to recognize that a clear business purpose was necessary to change action and improve business performance. Bank executives wanted to increase collaboration among lending staff and increase loan revenues through cross-selling. Researchers were hired to determine how collaboration was occurring and if technology was assisting in achieving tangible revenue goals. Findings of the research team indicated that e-mail showed little communication, let alone collaboration, among lending staff leading to cross-selling.[3] After the executives saw the results of the research, they decided to define objectives, change policies, and improve procedures to make collaboration important to staff. Sales goals for cross-selling were established for lending staff in real estate and commercial loans. Credit analysts were required to be included in the proposal stage of the lending process. These changes resulted in reductions in the cost of booking low quality loans and increased revenue from cross-selling to existing customers. Clear business objectives and formal incentives increased collaboration and use of existing technology, improving the bank's performance.

Establish Guiding Principles for Collaboration

Basic guiding principles for collaboration from key executives are critical to break the historical "gap" between the business and IT. General statements that there should be a "culture of collaboration" do not mean much without guiding principles. Executives should expect that shared and conflicting views always exist and that they can add to the success of technology initiatives. If staff observe individuals being isolated, demoted, or fired for voicing different views and raising questions, then collaboration is not feasible. In contrast, if staff from all functions and units with differing views are encouraged to raise issues, submit recommendations, and obtain approval of changes to initiatives, budgets, and performance measures, then an environment of collaboration for results exists.

In a large technology initiative for an electric utility, the sponsoring executive communicated guiding principles for collaboration at the outset of the multiyear effort. The following were guiding principles to be sustained over the entire period:

- A joint business-IT team is to work closely together from the launch of the initiative through the completion of all related projects.
- Individual performance plans should support the long-term partnership between the business and IT staff.
- New positions and resources will be provided to ensure that communication and collaboration is sustained across the organization for the term of the initiative.
- Consultants are part of the joint business-IT team. Consultants have authority to recommend, but corporate managers make the decisions.
- Differing viewpoints and even conflict should not be avoided; they should be addressed from a positive perspective to reduce risk and ensure initiative success.

Structuring Collaboration in a Single Business Unit

Organizational structure and boundary lines have a critical effect on collaboration success. Reporting lines, individual loyalty, and performance considerations drive how collaboration is actually conducted and what results are achieved. When executives understand that all reporting lines are barriers, they can identify the right processes and methods to increase collaboration across these barriers. Managers appreciate executives' support for collaboration to help build paths for staff to cross boundaries.

A single executive with direct reporting lines is the most basic collaborative structure, as illustrated in Figure 5.2. The executive defines or involves staff in developing the purpose, guidelines, and processes for effective collaboration. When the need for collaboration is clear, managers and staff are more able to rapidly establish relationships, share information, and fully develop exciting opportunities, while recognizing risks for technology. The executive must emphasize collaboration in performance planning and evaluation to ensure that staff take on the challenging aspects of collaboration.

A single executive collaboration structure is possible within all four of the management approaches described. The effectiveness of the collaboration depends on how the direct reports interact with the executive and with each other. The executive sets the model for the way differing viewpoints are treated. For example, if the executive wants only his viewpoint expressed, then direct reports are likely to reduce their inter-

Figure 5.2
Single Executive Collaboration Structure

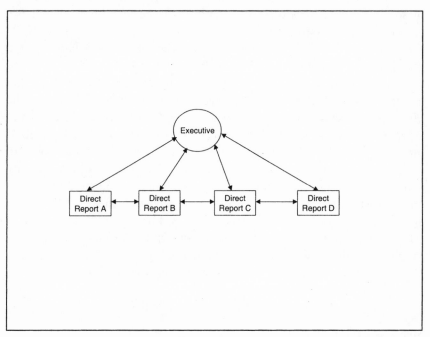

actions with him. Direct reports may infer from this attitude that collaboration is not acceptable. As a result, they will avoid collaboration and reinforce rigid barriers. If the executive is open to feedback and dissention, and staff are safe to express different views, collaboration will be likely to include more debate and negotiation.

Structuring Collaboration Among Multiple Business Units

Collaboration is challenging when more than one executive is responsible for a strategic technology initiative that involves multiple business units and functions. The collaboration structure for this circumstance must encompass many management levels and units across the organization, as illustrated in Figure 5.3. In this case it is essential for the executive to assess current collaboration practices and develop a framework for how collaboration must be conducted to achieve the business benefits of a technology initiative. Management levels, direct and dotted reporting lines, personal relationships, and politics do affect this form of collaboration. Complex, multilayered collaboration is common when technology must integrate operating information, transaction processing, and financial data across many functions in the organization. The effect of solid reporting lines on collaboration must be identified for collaboration to be successful.

Collaboration becomes more complex when executives consider the multilevel implications. In Chapter 3, Realizing the Strategic View of Technology, a readiness assessment was introduced that identifies what is needed for organizations to prepare for technology. Included in the business readiness assessment is an analysis of collaboration across many layers of the organization. This analysis is necessary to develop recommendations regarding the most effective way for various work groups to collaborate and achieve the business results. The collaboration capability and readiness analysis identifies what and how knowledge and experience from business units, vendors, and advisers must be shared to achieve the business outcomes of initiatives. For example, current methods of conducting meetings and completing initiative tasks are very appropriate if the new initiative is similar to prior technology efforts. However, if the new initiative requires changes in organizational struc-

Figure 5.3
Multilevel Collaboration Structure

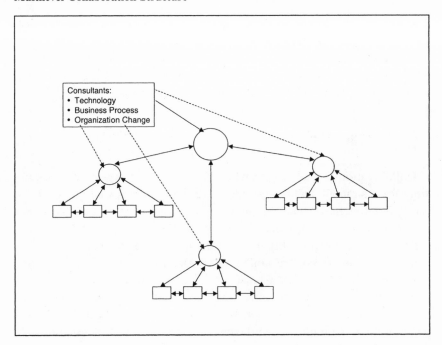

ture and staff reductions, then guiding principles for collaboration may have to change. Guidelines must include confidentiality requirements, processes for proposing and approving staff reductions, and modifications to the reporting structure. The forms of collaboration may vary. One organization may use formal offsite meetings, while another may use very informal, short, on-site conversations. Executives need to evaluate collaboration effectiveness over the course of the initiative. If collaboration is not contributing to achieving the business objectives, then modifications to the collaboration purpose statements, principles, and methods must occur.

It is important to emphasize that collaboration across functional boundaries and barriers is difficult, especially when unsupported by executives. Even high-performing, bold, and creative managers think long and hard before they risk crossing organization boundaries to lead mid-level collaboration. Often they believe their long-term career credibility, growth, and stability are at stake if they cross boundaries. To make collaboration across boundaries effective, executives must engage their peers and key managers in developing ground rules for initiating, conducting, and modifying collaboration across the organization. Once these are in place, communication should occur to ensure that any manager or staff member can cross these barriers without risk to conduct their initiative responsibilities.

A study at Hewlett-Packard in the mid-1990s identified the importance of organizational structure for collaboration and the role of executive support for the introduction of a new technology reuse method.[4] This study is a classic in highlighting the importance of active executive support for collaboration when introducing new methods in technology product development. The findings of the study indicate that when Hewlett-Packard began a reuse effort, it was not successful until an executive position was created at a level equal to other product development executives. The reuse executive created a clear vision, purpose, and process with his peers that enabled staff to effectively collaborate with the product development teams and obtain results. As a result, reuse experts had a clear role in the product development process and were not considered outsiders; nor were they thought to be extraneous resources. In contrast, other reuse specialists at Hewlett-Packard without this support were left to be lone advocates. Their effort to win support for reuse of technology by force of personality and individual initiative overwhelmed them and did not produce expected improvements to products or reduce time to market.

Executive-level accountability is essential for collaboration to generate business results from technology investments encompassing the multi-level structure. The executive leads in ensuring that the purpose, guiding principles, and methods for collaboration are clear and fit the business need. In addition, the executive is actively engaged in supporting ongoing communication and collaboration with peer executives. Collaboration frequently falls apart in all four of the management approaches when executives fail to make it a priority. A proactive executive keeps an eye on the collaboration and takes rapid action when necessary.

Structuring Collaboration Across Multiple Organizations

The structure for collaboration across multiple organizations for complex initiatives is the most challenging. Such initiatives often involve vendors, many business units, and outside consultants. Each participant must know how contacts are made and how information, confidentiality, and security are shared and maintained. The structure for how this collaboration should be developed when the technology initiative is approved is illustrated in Figure 5.4.

It is essential to outline the objectives and principles for collaboration in a written document and gain agreement up front. Many companies use organizational level agreements (OLAs) to control complex collab-

Figure 5.4
Structure for Cross-Organization Collaboration

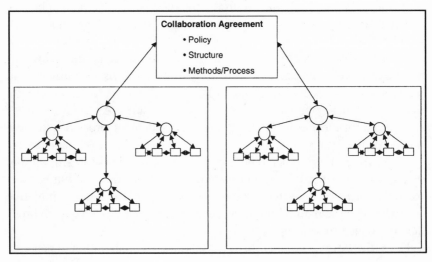

orations. These agreements state how organizations should work together and how disputes should be resolved, and they define the roles and commitment required from each organization. The agreements should outline how formal collaboration is conducted and how it affects contractual agreements and strategic business goals. Specifics on documentation, repositories, and informal communication channels can be developed later. Collaborative decision processes should be outlined in detail. Guidelines for sharing company information, decision making, and the process for escalation to executives from each organization should be outlined. The OLAs should also include the methods and resources available to encourage the collaboration that generates the creative and innovative ideas needed to add value.

Without a well-thought-out agreement, organizations encounter problems. For example, in a global payments processing organization, a product was jointly developed and maintained by a competing organization. A very brief contract with only a few lines on how to update the product was negotiated between the competing organizations for the technology development project. The product was implemented and some key customers reported dissatisfaction. After a number of years the larger payments organization wanted to investigate improving the product to meet customer needs. As a result of the vague intercompany agreement, a new project had to be initiated and resources from both companies involved in researching and determining a common course of action. After much time and expense, the larger company decided not to make any changes. A clearer contract could have saved resources and cost.

This formal structure for collaboration across multiple organizations is advisable for all management approaches for technology. Executives determine the level of risk their organizations can bear if critical errors, loss of customers, or a negative effect on business performance occurs. If the risk of failure is greater than the cost and effort of developing a collaboration agreement, it is worthwhile to develop the collaboration agreement.

PROCESSES AND METHODS FOR COLLABORATION

There are many defined and well-tested processes and methods that support effective collaboration to achieve business results. After many years of working on collaboration, we developed this general guideline: "When in doubt about the effectiveness of collaboration, put people together and find out what is really happening."

Structured Facilitated Meetings

A very useful approach to developing and maintaining effective collaboration in complex groups is structured facilitated meetings. These meetings are planned with management and participants to accomplish specific objectives and produce documented deliverables that directly support the initiative's goals. The meetings can last a few hours to a few days, depending on the urgency, complexity of the cost, objectives, deliverables, and availability of staff.

The benefits of using structured facilitated meetings with customer and end-user groups have been verified in research since the 1980s. IBM and Boeing researchers found that project schedules are shortened and product quality improved by using facilitated sessions with end users during the requirements development period. The joint application design method distributed by IBM is a notable product from the 1990s.[5] The joint application design method produced about a 40 percent reduction in the project life cycle. In the mid-1990s facilitated sessions were used for internal IT projects and rated as the most effective method for linking customer needs with technology development capabilities.[6] Since that time, methods from computer design and organizational development continue to be introduced to improve processes and tools aiding collaboration.

Visual Methods

Visual methods include storyboarding, high-level process charts, graphical modeling, and other simulations used to illustrate complex business processes and products and to generate innovative ideas for improving and evaluating their value. Many executives rarely get a "bird's eye view" of how their company works and gives value to customers. These high-level illustrations and simulations are created in collaborative working sessions with managers and experts from the business. The illustrations highlight the need for changes to policies, organization structure, business processes, operating controls, and metrics to increase the business results from technology. Management and staff then use the illustrations to aid in the detailed definition and implementation of technology. We have seen executives who are so excited by the storyboards that they want them posted in their offices.

Team Co-Location

Other methods to encourage collaboration are co-locating staff into the same work space. Frequently, the approach is to locate IT in the same area as the business units they are supporting. Another approach is to establish a "war room" or "bull pen" where everyone works in an open room without any cubicles. Both approaches encourage conversation and collaboration. The effectiveness of these approaches can be complemented by other methods and tools.

Technology Collaboration Tools

A recent method for improving collaboration is the use of technology collaboration tools. From reviewing research and industry experience, we can state that these tools do produce business benefits. In order for them to be effective there must be a specific business purpose, an understanding of the organizational structure, as well as defined processes and refinement phases to improve collaboration across organizations.[7] A recent research study compared the efforts of two global organizations to utilize technology tools for collaboration. The study first identified a bank as unsuccessful in improving collaboration because management focused on technical solutions. Different global regions never attempted to identify common needs or integrate practices and procedures. Individual regions built intranets and portals that had no connection globally. In a second successful case of a chemical corporation, challenges with technology tools for collaboration were encountered early. Management gradually refined the technology collaboration process and tools. Eventually the company decided to use facilitators to promote the effective use of the technology tool to share industry knowledge.

Collaboration Mapping

We found a number of studies using staff network maps and organizational assessments to evaluate the business benefits of using collaboration technology tools. Mapping collaboration and its value to the organization improves the measurement of business results. Large companies such as IBM, British Telecom, and Bristol-Myers Squibb have identified benefits of collaboration through a process that started with a mind map. A mind map illustrates a central idea and graphically expands it using the metaphor of a network of brain cells. Information from the individuals connected through this mind map was gathered to find out the benefits of collaboration of professionals working in the field of knowledge management. The major benefits of this collaboration are time savings in seeking and sharing information, reduced redundancy in problem solving, and decreased proposal development time from days to hours.[8] Other methods for tracking e-mail and call counts reveal how often collaboration occurs in organizations. This information reveals to management the most important opportunities for linking collaboration to results.

Here is an example of an organization collaboration map that became essential to the success of a large technology initiative with many individual product implementations and business process improvements. The initial map illustrated the importance of collaboration on an ongoing basis with managers and staff from many divisions. This collaboration process, organization-wide training, and technology implementation planning were all developed with participation from key decision makers and staff using the map illustrated in Figure 5.5.

The large circles on the top of the diagram identify the units in the organization that had the most influence on the success of the initiative. The small circles on the bottom of the diagram represent field transaction processing units that needed to be included in all of the projects and that required training and support. As the technology initiative progressed, it was efficient to have a full time manager responsible for communication

Figure 5.5
Technology Initiative Collaboration Map

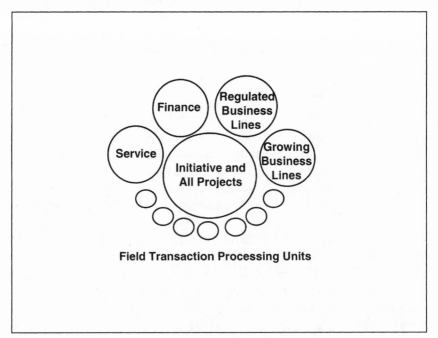

and collaboration. This manager was the first person notified of any issues or risks for business units. He made sure that senior managers'
questions were answered and issues were raised with the initiative sponsor. When the sponsor knew of changes in the business or executive
perspectives, he directed the manager to collaborate by soliciting options
to stay on track.

WHAT YOU CAN DO: SET THE MODEL FOR COLLABORATION

Executives can improve ongoing collaboration by being role models
with their peers and sharing their knowledge of external market conditions with others. With this information, initiative sponsors have timely
and critical information driving the company that then stimulates additional collaboration. Witnessing collaboration between executives encourages staff that previously avoided one another to see each other as
resources for meeting external demands. Collaboration among executives
is essential because managers and staff believe it is important only when
they see it occurring at the top.

SUMMARY

Effective collaboration within organizations is an essential element in
increasing business results from technology initiatives. Higher levels of
business performance are not achieved through general appeals to improve
collaboration. Definition of a clear business purpose for collaboration, ad-
herence to guiding principles, and selection and use of appropriate processes and methods ensure the realization of business results. Since
technology initiatives affect many parts of the organization and even multiple organizations, collaboration should be structured to counteract the
barriers that reporting lines support. The structure for collaboration must
be increasingly formal as technology initiatives involving a single executive with strategic accountability grow to encompass multiple levels of
executives and multiple organizations. Fortunately, many well-tested methods and tools are available to develop and maintain effective collaboration
for the duration of the initiatives.

QUESTIONS FOR REFLECTION AND DISCUSSION

1. How do you ensure that collaboration exists and is beneficial within
   your company?

2. How does your organization build paths to cross barriers and subcultures?

3. How constructively does your organization deal with conflict, differences of views, and sharing of ideas and information?

4. How can you communicate that different points of view aid good decision making, engender a better understanding of the company, and contribute to innovation for value?

5. How do you communicate a clear business purpose and guiding principles for organization-wide collaboration?

6. What methods and tools are available to support effective collaboration?

NOTES

1. Cross, R., N. Nohria, and A. Parket. "Six Myths About Informal Networks and How to Overcome Them." *MIT Sloan Management Review* (Spring 2002): 67–75.

2. Schrage, M. *Serious Play: How the World's Best Companies Simulate to Innovate.* Boston: Harvard Business School Press, 2000. The book in general describes how prototypes, simulations, and models improve products and productivity.

3. Cross, R., N. Nohria, and A. Parket. "Six Myths About Informal Networks and How to Overcome Them." *MIT Sloan Management Review* (Spring 2002): 72.

4. Fachamps D. "Organizational Factors and Reuse." *IEEE Software* (September 1994): 31–41.

5. Wood, J., and Denise Silver. *Joint Application Design: How to Design Quality Systems in 40% Less Time.* New York: John Wiley & Sons, 1989.

6. Keil, H., and E. Carmel. "Customer-Developer Links in Software Development." *Communications of the ACM* 38 (May 1995): 39.

7. Newell, S., S. Pan, R. Galliers, and J. Huang. "The Myth of the Boundaryless Organization." *Communications of the ACM* 44 (December 2001): 74–76.

8. Millen, D., M. Fontaine, and M. Muller. "Understanding the Benefit and Costs of Communities of Practice." *Communications of the ACM* 45 (April 2002): 69–73.

Chapter 6

DEVELOPING ORGANIZATION-WIDE TECHNOLOGY DECISION MAKING

Effective organization-wide decision making for technology can minimize vague and confusing accountability as described in the Chapter 1, Debunking the "Promise of Technology." Timely, well-informed decisions made at the right level of authority are critical to executing and implementing the business changes needed to derive measurable benefits. To improve business results from technology, an organization-wide approach to decision making must be in place over the entire course of initiatives. Decisions regarding initiatives that generate technology projects, budgets, and implementation plans are only the beginning. Any change in technology has a ripple effect across the organization. Business management and staff make many decisions concerning procedure modifications, job responsibilities, and logistics to support customer transactions. There are decisions about how technology is implemented that ensure that the business continues to operate.

This chapter describes the key elements of an organization-wide decision-making process. We outline how companies can establish and develop this decision-making process into an efficient mechanism to improve the success rate of critical initiatives and sustain a focus on business benefit. Tables are provided that reveal the decisions necessary at the formation, implementation, and completion of initiatives. To illustrate how this decision-making process works, a case is presented later in the chapter to illustrate how companies can identify, research, and resolve critical decisions within any timeframe to meet any challenge.

THE NEED FOR ORGANIZATION-WIDE TECHNOLOGY DECISIONS

An organization-wide process for decision making should outline *why, what, when, who,* and *how* decisions are made to derive benefits and effective technology usage. A clear structure for decision making is not enough to eliminate vague and confusing accountability for business results. The decision-making process should connect all management levels, profit and cost centers, staff, and functional units directly or indirectly affected by the technology change. Decision-making models, process steps, and patterns of action must be relevant to the organization, power relationships, and operating practices. Management commitment to utilize the decision process across the organization is critical. The decision-making processes should be supported by accurate and meaningful information on customer behavior, staff use of technology, and the effect of new technologies on the existing technology infrastructure. Lastly, this information must be available to staff, analysts, managers, and decision makers as it is needed.

The decision-making process, methods, and tools should be documented and be easily accessible because many parallel efforts occur during technology initiatives. These parallel efforts include:

- Monitoring strategic initiatives
- Overseeing multiple projects related to technology or business operations and an initiative
- Tracking and controlling budgets
- Ensuring that customer relationships remain stable or are strengthened
- Purchasing technology and professional services
- Redesigning and implementing business processes across the organization
- Integrating projects with measurable business benefits

Why are organization-wide decisions needed for technology initiatives? Organization-wide decisions are needed because the outcomes of technology decisions can affect business performance. A significant number of strategic decisions affect parallel work in multiple business units and ultimately business performance. Often when strategic decisions are delegated, the resulting outcomes are based on short-term project goals and not on overall customer and business benefits. An organization-wide decisionmaking process is required to ensure that strategic decisions are identified, researched, and examined from a broader business perspective and that they support the strategic or critical business objectives. These decisions require tough trade-offs and often the wrong decision can have a negative impact on business performance. Internal staff input is needed to raise issues and influence good decision making. Outside resources may also be needed to provide specific expertise, analysis, and advice to assist in these difficult decisions.

Following is a case of a global electronics company that made decisions too hastily and without checking on how these decisions would affect business performance. Corporate headquarters in Japan decided to implement an enterprise resource planning system, using the SAP product, worldwide. To support this effort, the U.S. division immediately took staff off their jobs, moved them to the east coast, and assigned them to the project. This hasty decision provided little time to complete a thorough business analysis of the effects of new technology on profit and cost centers. The team was so time constrained and pressured that it even rejected an offer of assistance from a West Coast profit center that had already implemented a different version of the same system. The implementation progressed until a conflict between software versions was identified. This conflict added time and risk of errors to the order entry process. The team had little time to investigate the risk of this issue and decided to move forward with implementation of the system. The new system caused the West Coast profit center to experience a reduction in order entry efficiency. This case is an example of a strategic decision that, when examined from a broader business perspective, met corporate objectives but led to more work for some units.

Decisions that contributed to the reduction of benefits for this technology investment include:

- Moving unprepared teams to a new location
- Deciding on an aggressive implementation schedule without evaluating the effect on the quality of implementation
- Not supporting a thorough business operations and risk analysis
- Not utilizing all available expertise
- Deciding to implement software programs without measuring the risk to local business units

How Could Organization-Wide Decision Making Change This Case?

Organization-wide decision making helps ensure that the appropriate person makes an informed decision at the proper time. In this case, let's assume corporate made the appropriate decision to change to new enterprise technology. The next decision—to move staff—apparently did not take into consideration the time it would take to prepare staff for their assignments and to conduct effective nationwide research. If corporate had asked management to analyze the effect on existing work of allocating existing staff to this project, if they had asked the division already experienced with the SAP product for advice on implementation and use, the business results of the implementation may have been different. Using rapid decision making without analyzing the business impact, can often lead to high-risk situations and reduced success.

Ownership of the decisions and accountability for results must be associated with the appropriate level of executive and middle management. In Chapter 4, Building Organization-Wide Processes for Delivering Value from Technology, we presented a model for accountability that affects business value. Executives are accountable for making strategic decisions about the infrastructure, its effect on business performance, customer loyalty, and value. Only the most strategic decisions or issues that add opportunity or risk to the technology investment and business should be escalated to the executive level.

Senior managers have organization-wide accountability for decisions that affect multiple business units and/or functions responsible for technology initiatives. They have a common interest in determining reporting structure, work processes, and technology to sustain and grow the value of the company. Senior managers make the decisions for company, local business line, and functional needs for technology functionality. Middle managers make decisions on technology after confirming that there is great benefit and little risk of affecting other business units, corporate data, and processes. Local accountability decisions are limited to technology improvements affecting single business units, profit centers, or functional areas.

Timing of Decisions

Timing of decisions is critical to supporting the realization of business benefits from technology initiatives. Figure 6.1 illustrates three time frames that drive decisions needed across the business. The first time frame for decision making is when the technology initiative is presented and approved for action. The second time frame for decision making guides the progress of the initiatives from launch through completion. This time frame can extend for weeks, months, and for major strategic technology initiatives into years. The third time frame for decision making is at the completion of the initiative and focuses on the benefits the organization achieved. Decisions are necessary in the last time frame to further improve the initiative and processes to improve the business results.

Serious problems occur when decisions are not made at the right time in the initiative and when they are made with inadequate or incorrect information. Managing the flow of good information and the timing of decisions with the implementation plans for specific projects and work efforts is challenging. Often work continues on technology projects even when critical decisions are delayed. In some cases delays of just days or hours can become critical. Such delays in decision making add risk to the projects, business results, and benefits. Therefore, any organization-wide decision process must have an administrative structure for communication and risk management. The structure should have tools to generate red flags when decisions are delaying critical work, and research and analysis to develop recommendations and make decisions is inadequate.

Decisions Made at Initiative Launch

Identifying what decisions have to be made in the right time frame is a constant effort that steering groups, middle managers, and project teams aggressively pursue from initiative launch to implementation of technology. Table 6.1 identifies *which* decisions are best made on an organization-wide level when technology initiatives are formed.

Column one, Decision makers, identifies the recommended decision makers who participate in the formation of a technology initiative. Column two, Technology, identifies decisions required for the initiative and a product development, system integration, or other technology-driven effort. Column three, Organizational Change, identifies recommendations to management on how the business must change to take advantage of the new technology. Recommendations come from a variety of sources include internal management and staff, change management, quality specialists, or other specialists. Column four, Business Benefits, identifies the decisions and actions that divisions, cost-center, and profit-center management make to prepare and use new technology to deliver benefits. The decisions that business managers make are frequently not standardized, formalized, or documented unless it is required. These decisions can vary based on the technology, business practices, customer relationship management practices, and market conditions.

Each row of this table highlights critical opportunities, trade-offs, and risks that decision makers must be prepared to address. In column two,

Figure 6.1
Timing of Technology Decisions

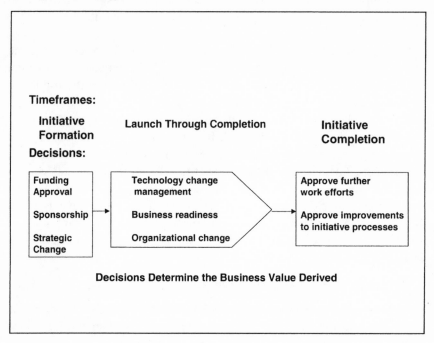

Technology, for example, an executive decision is to approve the target business benefits required from technology. Other decisions executives make or oversee are to fund technology investments and their related projects. These decisions should be based on written business cases with costs and benefits estimated and validated.

At the initiative formation executives should also make a decision on whether the technology encompasses organizational change. New technology might offer an opportunity for executives to direct management to evaluate and recommend changes to organizational structure, business processes, and staff competencies to improve business performance. If organizational changes are to be considered, then staff must know this early to manage them within the scope of the initiative. In addition, middle managers must know their level of authority for influencing and making decisions about change. When organizational change is made part of a high-priority initiative, executives can obtain expert advise from internal or external professionals skilled in organizational change, quality improvement, or other approaches to determine a course of action and establish change processes. When decisions on change are made early,

Table 6.1
Decisions at the Formation of Technology Initiatives

Decision Makers	Technology	Organizational Change	Business Benefits
Executives	Approve strategic technology initiatives Fund technology projects Appoint sponsors and set objectives in performance objectives Identify time frame for delivery of results	Recommend evaluation and design of strategic organizational changes • Structures • Competencies • Processes • Patterns of action • Recognition	Approve strategic business initiatives Fund business readiness programs Commit and acquire resources Determine frequency and level of status for initiatives Select business metrics for initiative benefits
Executive Sponsors Senior and All Affected Managers	Decisions affecting infrastructure: • Policy changes • Data entry and integrity • Processes that directly effect the technology • Results of implementations • Issue Reporting	Recommendations on change management plans for cross-functional environment: • New business process designs • New functional relationships • New forms of customer interaction • New patterns of action	Create the process for decisions on cross-functional actions: • Define business process, policies and procedures • Operating structure • Positions • Operating metrics • Performance standards • Reporting
Management Sponsor Functional Managers	Approve scope of the projects: • Track and manage budget • Manage resources • Periodic review of project and changes	Recommend change management plans based on project scope: • Business managers • Customers and external parties • Other organization stakeholders	Create process for decisions affecting business units, functions: • Policy • Operations issues • Reduction of business risks • Business benefits compare estimate to actual

management and staff have the time to conduct the research, analyze, and build organization-wide commitment to drive the changes forward. A note of caution: When organizational change issues are excluded from technology initiatives, changes to business processes are often tactical and important business performance opportunities are missed. One chief financial officer said, "We paved the same old cow path," referring to new technology that was implemented but produced little productivity improvement or business benefit.

One of the most critical decisions executives make at initiative formation is to approve and fund a business-readiness assessment for technology. When the cost and risk of technology is high, establishing business readiness reduces the risks to business performance. The cost of a readiness assessment should be weighed against the risk of customer dissatisfaction, staff productivity loss, and the effect of breakdowns and backlogs on mission-critical business processes.

The second row outlines the decisions that senior and middle managers make when establishing processes and practices to be used in the execution of technology and business projects related to initiatives. As initiatives cross many divisions, units, and functions, these decision processes become critical or initiatives flounder. Technology projects define their own decision processes. Decision processes for change management must define and involve all managers directly and indirectly affected. These processes should outline how detailed decisions for specific projects are to be presented and negotiated among middle management and how the most strategic decisions are to be escalated to executives. Steering groups and sponsorship roles must be defined clearly and their decisions outlined. Here are some of the important considerations:

- Ensure that the business objectives of the initiative are met.
- Make decisions to resolve critical issues and engage all key stakeholders.
- Clarify and support the priority of the initiative.
- Oversee the planned progress of the initiative.
- Take action if technical or business risks to benefits are identified.
- Offer direction when business conditions change.

The third row in this table describes the need for management sponsors and functional managers making decisions for individual technology projects, change management advisors, and business units directly affected by initiatives to define their decision processes. These decision processes should involve end user representatives and managers when operating policies and procedures are changed.

What You Can Do for Initiatives: Make Sure That a Business Case Is Developed

All technology initiatives should be supported by a business case. Business case methods and criteria are well established. The basic business case typically includes:

- Description of the proposed business strategy, scope, and expected outcome
- Recommendation for how technology can be used to meet the business need
- Description of supporting market data, business process analysis, and technology capabilities to deliver the desired results
- Preliminary budget, resources, and time frames required to execute the initiative
- Risk assessment of the initiative and its effects on the business
- Preliminary phased implementation plan
- Estimated financial returns using company tools and formulas

Before final decisions regarding technology are made, the business cases for technology investments require extensive analysis, and customer and user needs should be validated. Not requiring a thorough business analysis and feasibility study adds risk to realizing desired business results. In a thorough business case preparation, all opportunities and risks are identified and presented in supporting documentation.

What Else You Can Do: Require a Technology Initiative Risk Assessment

It is essential that a risk assessment be performed for all technology initiatives. The risk assessment should include all related projects and should specify their anticipated effects on the business. Too often the risk assessment step is skipped because managers are too focused on winning the budget. Executives must ask for risk assessments to ensure technology initiatives' effects on the company are identified and managed. A thorough assessment includes identification of the risks, calculation of the probability of the risks occurring, and estimation of the impact the risks could have on the business. The degree of risk is typically ranked as high, medium, or low. Here is a scenario that illustrates how to think about technology risk. The key risk identified for a proposed technology initiative is delay in deriving benefits because the technology product takes a long time to implement. Based on discussions with users of the product, decision makers confirm that the technology does take time to implement and could disrupt ongoing business. They concluded that the probability of risk and its impact on the business are both high. Company officials calculate the risk of departments being disrupted and company information being lost or erroneous. Executives take the risk assessment and make decisions as to how much risk they are willing to take. They identify when action should be taken to mitigate the risk.

DECISIONS MADE WHILE INITIATIVES ARE IN PROGRESS

When initiatives are in progress, executives and managers should expect to make many decisions concerning how the organization must change and what business processes must be modified to derive benefits from new technology. Decisions concerning changes to implementation schedules, budgets, and phase deliverables require steering groups, sponsors, or departments to review and assess their effects. Decisions regarding financial, legal, marketing, policy, procedures, and information management issues may also arise as a result of the initiative. Other decisions related to business readiness to adapt to new technology and modified business processes must be made to ensure business benefits are delivered. Table 6.2 identifies many, but not all, of the decisions that must be made during an initiative implementation.

Table 6.2 outlines the most critical decisions that need to be made while initiatives are in progress. Executives make critical go/no-go decisions for large projects based on timely and accurate information. This information reveals changing conditions that could cause the technology initiatives to lose value. When conditions change, executives must decide to cancel, restart, or modify the investment and its benefits. If the initiatives are critical to company performance, these decisions must be made rapidly to address the risks, identify triggers for action, and intensify reviews until the initiative is progressing as desired. Identifying the decisions that have to be made under different conditions ensures that executives know what they need to do to keep the initiative progressing to completion.

Decisions on organizational change management must be made as early as possible during initiative implementation. Organizational change advisors, business management, and staff representatives analyze and recommend critical changes. The recommendations with broad effects on business operations have strategic importance and require executive approval. Examples of strategic decisions include changes in reporting structure, staff responsibilities, and business process improvement that affect business performance. Executives overseeing a large technology initiative approved a recommendation from the business sponsor to improve the long-term results of a financial initiative by shifting the reporting of the payroll unit from human resources to the controller's

Table 6.2
Decisions for Initiatives in Progress

Decision Makers	Technology	Organizational Change	Business Benefits
Executives	Go/No-Go decisions on large, critical strategic technology initiatives: • Budget changes • Scope additions • Schedule delays Confirm benefits still can be realized Stop projects that no longer deliver benefits	Recommend critical changes requiring executive approval: • Policy changes • Process improvement • Staff responsibilities • Performance requirements • Skill development	Decisions on high-priority business issues that affect: • Customer behavior • Operating performance metrics & measures • Changes affecting staff • Business risks • Validate or revise business benefits estimates

Executive Sponsors
Senior Managers
All Affected Managers
	Decisions on organization-wide issues:
	
	• Policies for quality of data & correction
	• Business process changes driven by new technology
	• Scope of deliverables for
	  - Business reporting requirements
	  - System integration requirements & management decisions
		Recommendations on organization-wide changes:
		
		• Modification of major business processes
		• Staff effectiveness
		• Staff performance
			Decisions on organization-wide processes affecting:
			
			• Customers
			• Staff positions & skills required
			• Mission-critical activities
			• Business contingency plans

Management Sponsor **Functional Managers**	Go/No-Go decisions on milestones and/or phase transitions Decisions to resolve technical risks and issues Decisions for project changes such as scope, schedule, resources	Recommendations on high, medium and low priority organizational change issues affecting individuals and business units only	Decisions on unit operating readiness Define processes and procedures Approval of implementation plans, training and contingency plans

department. The shift was made because staff from the controller's department had the skills to improve the accounting controls for the entire payroll system. The decision was communicated quickly to the initiative steering group and a new payroll manager from the controller's department was added.

Organization-wide issues can be some of the most complex and sensitive to manage. These decisions are outlined in the second column,

Technology, of Table 6.2. Business sponsors with organization-wide accountability for decisions must balance the tension among the goals at the corporate level, the initiative objectives, and the projects linked to it. For executives to be successful at making organization-wide decisions, they must have experience in evaluating information from different business or functional perspectives, integrating recommendations that reconcile local and organization-wide needs, and ensuring completion of large enterprise technology initiatives. Engaging appropriate staff from technology, change management, and business operations improves the quality of these complex decisions. Often two parallel decision-making processes are needed. One process is to move technology projects ahead as quickly as possible; another is for managers to explore their complex business issues. In order for the initiative to continue, business management decisions must be coordinated with and support the technology implementation schedule. Business managers can be required to make decisions monthly, weekly, or even daily to ensure that all initiatives progress towards their agreed upon implementation dates.

The fourth column of Table 6.2, Business Benefits, outlines decisions that are very detailed and may affect jobs and project tasks. This column identifies some decisions made by middle management regarding the technology project and business unit readiness needs. The importance of these decisions should not be underestimated because critical omissions, errors, or misinterpretation of data elements could negatively affect business performance. The decisions about how to rectify issues and errors identified must be escalated to middle management or executive levels based on the magnitude of the risk to business performance.

DECISIONS AT THE COMPLETION OF TECHNOLOGY INITIATIVES

When technology initiatives are completed, it is necessary to evaluate the benefits realized. The process to evaluate, measure, and accurately interpret the benefits delivered should continue for 12 to 18 months after implementation. For example, an internal service unit implemented call center tracking software to reduce average call times and improve customer satisfaction. In the first 6 months after implementation, reports from the new customer service system proved that average call times were cut in half. Letters praising the high level of service were received. Management continued to track customer satisfaction for a full year and found that call times were further reduced in the next 6-month period. If management had only tracked results for the first few months, it may have missed the continued improvement in call times and the customer satisfaction this initiative delivered.

Table 6.3 outlines the decisions needed after initiatives are completed. A formal executive review of the outcomes of initiatives determines if the business, technology, and operating objectives were achieved and if any further action is necessary. The completion review of technology initiatives can generate new ideas and business opportunities to improve the customer experience, operations, and business performance. Recommendations can be prioritized and the resources can be assigned to begin research or implement them. An example of making decisions to improve initiatives based on reviews is a company with a history of difficulty in implementing technology initiatives. At a review of a completed initiative that was successful, executives decided to improve staff implementation skills. The executives decided to develop and deliver a training course to transfer the most effective tools for business analysis, project task completion, and collaboration skills. Over 200 staff from the company were trained.

If, after implementing technology, unprepared operations and staff cause negative effects to the business, executives must make rapid de-

Table 6.3.
Decisions after Technology Initiatives Are Completed

Decision Makers	Technology	Organizational Change	Business Benefits
Executives	Approve improvements to strategic technology and execution processes Recognize successes	Recommend improvements to change management processes	Approve improvements to business operations or line Approve analysis tools for customer tracking and business metrics for benefits
Executive Sponsors Senior Managers All Affected Managers	Decide if functional deliverables met success criteria Approve improvements to technology project processes	Recommend improvements to change management processes and decision methods	Measure business benefits achieved Identify further work efforts Approve improvements to initiative's processes
Management Sponsor Functional Managers	Approve improvements to technology system Recommend improvements on technology project execution	Recommend improvements in change management for projects	Decide on business operations improvements for new technology Recommend improvements on technology initiatives and business benefits

cisions to minimize negative effects to business performance. Too often executives think that three to six months of disruption to the business is normal after technology is implemented. If an effective decision-making process, business-readiness program, and executive oversight have been in place over the entire course of the initiative, then there is little likelihood of interruption of customer transaction activities, business processes, and market perceptions.

At the unit and functional level, there are numerous decisions required to fine-tune technology systems and business operations for months after implementation. The decision process should remain in place until all issues are resolved and business operational processes are running smoothly. During this post initiative period, analysis of system reports and staff usage of technology must be reviewed to determine what benefits and improvements were actually achieved. Often interviews and surveys of customers and staff are used as quantitative data included in the evaluation of results.

WHAT YOU CAN DO NOW: ESTABLISH AN ORGANIZATION-WIDE DECISION-MAKING PROCESS

Earlier we said that organization-wide decision making means that the appropriate person makes a well-informed decision at the required time. In order for this to happen, a process must be in place that identifies decision-making criteria and supports decision reviews. The business-readiness assessment outlined in Chapter 3, Realizing the Strategic Value of Technology, should include an evaluation of how an organization currently makes decisions for technology. The following are questions to ask:

- What is the current decision process? Is it effectively and consistently used, and how widely is it applied?
- What is working and not working in the decision-making process?
- How do you know if decisions achieve desired results?
- How do you know if the right people are making the right decisions?
- What management and staff capabilities are needed to make good decisions for technology investments?
- How are decisions on technology, projects, and business operations conducted over the entire course of initiatives?
- How are effective decisions recognized and rewarded?

Ask these questions to executives, managers, and all staff to find out how and where effective or ineffective decision making is occurring. After this information is obtained, strategies and plans to improve the effectiveness of the decision-making process can be developed.

An effective organization-wide process generates timely and well-informed decisions. The methods and tools selected must fit with the business and organization's operating practices. They must also have relevancy to the business outcomes. In some cases, staff must be trained to conduct research and fine-tune recommendations for executives who make very difficult and sensitive decisions. Staff also need time to practice how to use the methods and tools effectively for different technology initiatives. When the decision processes and skills are in place, they must be used constantly. Finally, staff must be recognized and rewarded for making decisions that result in successfully completed initiatives with measurable business results.

Decision making can be efficient and effective by taking small and consistent steps. Six months of consistent effort should result in improvements in business cases, benefit and cost estimates, and decision quality. Steps that have helped organizations are:

- Simplify the business case, analysis, and risk assessment, and require them for medium-to-high priority technology initiatives. Insist that benefit estimates are linked to observable and measurable staff action and customer behavior.

- Review priorities monthly with stakeholders for in-progress initiatives. Focus on five or fewer requests for priority change decisions at a single time.

- Ensure executive approval for decision-making policies regarding technology initiatives.

- Document and track all decisions surrounding technology initiatives.

- Provide a feedback mechanism for improvements to the decision process and tools.

- Introduce improvements to the decision process gradually.

- Recognize and reward effective decision making.

SUMMARY

Accountability for technology initiative decisions must be defined by organization level, timing, and effect on business performance. Many decisions are required over the course of initiatives. Decisions may be organized by implementation stages: initiation, in-progress, or completion. Quality decisions are critical to realizing the value of technology initiatives. An organization-wide process is necessary to ensure that well informed decisions are made at the appropriate level and that the decision-making process includes the key managers who represent business units that will be directly and indirectly affected by the technology and business process changes. Executives have a significant role in ensuring that structure, resources, and recognition are in place to support timely, informed, and high-quality technology decisions. When executives and managers experience the benefits of organization-wide decision making, they realize that they have a capability to successfully implement technology and derive measurable benefits.

QUESTIONS FOR REFLECTION AND DISCUSSION

1. How is information gathered for technology business cases and decisions?

2. Do you validate the relevancy and data of financial projections and formulas used to support technology decisions?

3. How do decisions for business processes and procedures ensure benefits from technology?

4. What organizational structure, processes, and competencies are needed to make good decisions for technology investments?

5. How do you know if completed technology initiatives are delivering projected business results?

Part III

THE NEW WAY TO GENERATE
VALUE FROM TECHNOLOGY

Chapter 7

ESTABLISHING A VALUE-DRIVEN MANAGEMENT PROCESS FOR TECHNOLOGY

The historical role of executive management is to create and grow the value of the business. Disciplines within the company, such as project management and software development, assume that management also knows how to create and grow value with technology. Executive management assumes that project management will align the project-related activities with the initiatives generated from business needs. These assumptions may or may not be correct.

We have found that it is challenging to establish consistent practices and processes that bring business and technology management together to use technology to derive business value. In advising business sponsors and their managers during large technology efforts such as enterprise resource management and merger integration, we have found that executives and managers are often surprised that they have roles and responsibilities for deriving value from technology. Business managers are surprised that they have to preserve the link between the technology and business objectives. Technology managers are often unaware that their role includes achieving business objectives and value. Why do these inconsistencies exist?

It appears that in most organizations, the responsibility for defining, communicating, and delivering value from technology investments is unclear. It is apparent that something is needed to reach managers on single projects as well as hundred of managers and their staffs across the company to assist them in achieving measurable value from all their technology-related efforts. Executives also need to know that managers are thinking strategically and leading action on technology initiatives that will meet business success criteria.

In this chapter we present the Seeing Solutions Map,[1] a framework and tool developed by Project Concepts, Inc., that clarifies and supports management processes and practices for achieving business objectives from technology investments. This map helps all levels of management communicate to staff about the business value objectives for technology initiatives that further define and implement the organization's strategic initiatives. In addition, the map ensures that management decision criteria for value creation and growth drive the implementation of technology. It supports productive collaboration among all business and technical viewpoints on the value of technology to customers and the entire organization. The map reveals the critical business actions and priorities needed to focus on delivering value.

The map was developed in response to lessons learned from large technology investments and as an easy way to assist clients and educate future managers who are currently students in business and technology. Data used in the design of the map was drawn from strategic initiatives to replace aging legacy systems, redesign high-volume transaction processing systems, implement enterprise resources planning technology, and complete merger integration efforts in a number of industries. The map format has continued to evolve since its presentation in 1996.[2]

The key value of the Seeing Solutions Map is that it provides executives and managers with a way to coordinate research, business plans, decisions, and changes with formal project management methodologies. Using the map, managers can communicate a clear message in basic business language about why an initiative is being implemented. It allows managers and staff to know the process for business-issue resolution and to measure the effects decisions have on projects. The map coordinates activities across the organization over the course of the initiative. Finally, the map highlights the responsibilities that the business has for deriving value from technology that are outside the scope of project management.

THE SEEING SOLUTIONS MAP

The Seeing Solutions Map demands vigilance about the trade-offs required to generate value over the course of strategic business initiatives. The most successful initiatives set high objectives for value and quality while closely managing benefits, costs, and risks. The final design of the

Seeing Solutions Map was drawn from executives who led critical strategic initiatives and were successful in delivering specific business benefits to customers. These executives were clear from the outset of their technology initiatives that business value criteria would drive overall success. In other words, business value was the definition for success. Therefore, a statement of business value and decision criteria is at the core of the map. We call this statement the value proposition, which is the definition of success for the initiative. The Seeing Solutions Map also encourages innovation not just in product and technology development but also in structure, management policy, and practices as a support for organization-wide business process integration and productivity improvement.

The phrases value proposition and return on investment have become buzzwords and do not always have a specific meaning when related to business objectives, technology investments, and risks. Without agreement on what value really means to an organization, collaboration among executives and managers may be confusing. In some management groups, everyone has a different definition of the value proposition for an initiative or a business function. Group members realize that they must resolve these different views of value before they can communicate with executives and obtain functional agreement to increase the success of technology initiatives.

The value proposition statement of a technology initiative provides the link to strategic plans, business plans, and objectives. When the overriding initiative is clear about how business value will be generated, the business sponsor, project manager, and managers affected by the technology for each related project have the means to stay linked to the value proposition of the initiative. A clear business value proposition statement is a powerful tool to gain agreement for both tangible and intangible value and to identify the effects of the technology on the business. Value is always a trade-off between business opportunity and risk. A single financial formula cannot capture the short- and long-term value that technology offers.

A specific business value proposition statement should be established for all technology initiatives and execution projects. At the center of the Seeing Solutions Map, as presented in Figure 7.1, is what we call the value circle. The value circle is a very brief summary of the value proposition statement for the initiative. The top three business opportunities for the initiative are listed in priority order in the upper half of the circle. The top three risks associated with achieving these business opportunities are listed in order of significance at the lower half of the circle. Dividing the circle is the "survival line," which identifies the business criteria used to determine whether the whole initiative and specific opportunities are viable. Business criteria for the survival line can be financial (a break-even point), customer driven (satisfaction and retention rates), or productivity and quality measures. The survival line criteria must be relevant to the business value that the initiative is expected to create.

The outer circle of the map is a ring of actions by the business that is divided into five regions. Each region of the outer ring describes a key action that is critical to the business results of the initiative. The five actions that must occur are

1. Conduct inquiry
2. Create concept
3. Build a model or prototype

Figure 7.1
The Seeing Solutions Map

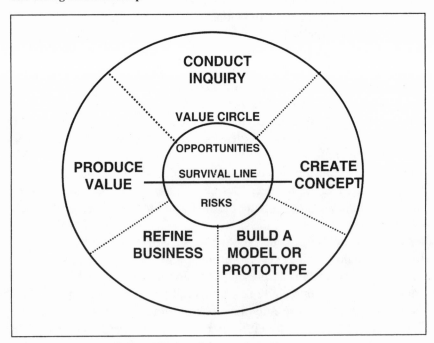

Printed with the permission of Project Concepts, Inc.

4. Refine business
5. Produce value

The dividing lines between each region are dotted to indicate that actions often occur in parallel. Prior actions regarding connecting activities from different regions should be reevaluated when business value from the initiative is questionable or when business conditions change. For example, customer needs discovered when conducting an inquiry might generate new concepts for business process improvements as well as decision criteria for the survival line.

Many established methods for technology implementation are linear and organize tasks. Other methods are iterative, which emphasize speed to market at times over other business considerations. These methods do not always support business initiative concerns. The reality is that technology initiatives frequently need to adjust assumptions, requirements, priorities, and design during testing and installation. In addition, management priorities frequently change and initiatives have to be updated rapidly to generate business value. When methods are rigidly linear, or too narrowly focused, teams are not encouraged to revise early assumptions; important opportunities to tailor technology to achieve business goals may be missed.

The Seeing Solutions Map is primarily a management tool. The map allows managers to think, analyze, and revisit decisions if business value is at risk over the course of an initiative. In addition, the map helps business management identify when and how operating policy, organizational structure, and staff performance affect value derived from technology investments. The map documents business priorities encouraging managers with different professional perspectives and responsibilities to collaborate across boundaries for the benefit of the entire organization.

We have found that most business managers will agree to involvement in an initiative to increase business value. The map allows managers to share their strengthens and business knowledge to have a positive effect on technology investments. When managers participate in more than one initiative that produces measurable business results, they transfer the learning to future initiatives. Through this learning process for deriving business value from technology investments, companies can find ways to improve overall company capability to achieve measurable results from technology.

Collaborative teams or task forces use the Seeing Solutions Map to create a "business target" for results from technology. Each initiative task force or collaborative team determines the top two or three activities that management must oversee to completion in every region of the map to deliver business benefits and results. These teams review the map monthly or even weekly, if necessary, modifying it in response to changing conditions or priorities. In our experience, business and technology staff are drawn together into intense and exciting discussions about the value circle when they realize that they have an important role in contributing value to the business.

THE SEEING SOLUTIONS MAP IN ACTION

Let's see how applying the Seeing Solutions Map shifts the organization-wide conversation from implementing technology products and projects to deriving business value from technology. The map is used in three stages:

1. Prior to approval of initiatives and projects or acquisition of products and services
2. While initiatives are in progress
3. After initiatives and projects are completed and recognition of business benefits occurs

By applying the tool in these three stages, we illustrate the range of activities, how collaboration shifts to a focus on value and the decisions that have to be managed across an organization to fully realize measurable benefits.

To illustrate the use of the Seeing Solutions Map let's look at the hypothetical case of a customer service initiative in a medium-sized company. Customers are submitting complaints through a Web site and are waiting two or three days for responses from customer service. The Web site itself is fast, but the backend processes are slow and many manual tasks are linked to old legacy systems. An initiative is launched to integrate the front- and back-end systems to increase productivity and shorten customer response time. Executive management is aware that investments in major upgrades and replacement of legacy systems should be considered. The chief financial officer, chief information officer, and executive vice president of operations have identified a task force and have communicated the importance of the initiative and the need for productive collaboration. Task force goals are to identify all the issues and find ways to strengthen mutually beneficial relationships with customers and increase the value of the company.

The initiative task force uses the Seeing Solutions Map to manage the preproject approval stage. The task force focuses on the value circle and specifically on the conduct inquiry and create concept regions of the map. After some discussion, the task force decides that the top three topics that require research within the conduct inquiry region are (1) customer experiences with complaints, (2) current business processes, and (3) existing technology used in handling complaints. The task force identifies work teams for technology, business, and finance to research these topics. Technology team members are directed to assess current technologies and identify new options for products and tools. Business team members analyze existing business processes, customer satisfaction, and retention levels, as well as the long-term effects of technology change on the business. Financial analysis teams gather data from prior initiative proposals and projects to make recommendations for evaluating the tangible and intangible value of any solution.

Using the conduct inquiry region of the Seeing Solutions Map, investigation is conducted into the state of the current business and organizational capability to generate value in new ways with technology. The task force agrees to commit to inquiry activities to get a broader perspective on the initiative before forming concepts for potential solutions. Task force members understand how hard it is to hold back from leaping to a solution, but they have learned from prior experience that staying open and curious in the inquiry stage has led to greater breakthroughs. This leads them to develop a few questions that they believe may never have been asked before about customers and their business needs. Questions considered essential to ask the organization are:

- Which customers are making complaints?
- How can we secure their loyalty?
- How can we increase value for our customers?
- What in the current process is creating the delays that affect customers?
- Have we tried to improve this process before?
- If so, what was the result?

Work teams are encouraged to ask challenging questions and use tested tools to obtain the answers in a professional manner from customers, staff, and other resources. The executives of the company recognize that insightful questions lead to the most valuable business opportunities. Conversely, they recognize that marginal questions lead to marginal results, if not failure, for the initiative.

The task force works with regional sales managers to conduct a survey of customers to identify complaints. They also work with call center managers to conduct end-user interviews and observe the entire complaint management process. Meanwhile business analysts under the IT function are conducting a technology feasibility analysis for a customer service initiative using information on current customer complaints. Analysts find that the vast majority of complaints are researched, they are corrected immediately, and the customer is quickly contacted. However, a much smaller portion of complaints requires extensive research and cannot be corrected until an entire case history is developed, which causes the customer response time to be very long. Analysts find that current systems are not gathering information efficiently. Call center statistics are gathered by each technology system, and it is not possible to get a complete picture of how technology and staff work together to benefit the customer. This leads the team to conduct a brief analysis of the customer experience across sales, fulfillment, and service. The analysis uses a small sample of customers that could generate a higher quality of information than the inefficient and erroneous data from the fragmented systems.

A working session is scheduled for all teams and selected representatives from the business to create improvement concepts. Call center management and staff are invited to participate in forming the concepts of how their functions will operate in the future. Findings and conclusions from each work team are shared to ensure that all participants have the same information. The group uses a storyboard, a visual picture, to document the concepts for how customers, end users, and technology could better work together in the future to generate benefits. The group knows this method can help illustrate the full picture of how technology supports staff productivity, as well as customer relationships and satisfaction with products, service, and technology. A compelling vision for a self-service customer experience and complaint process emerges.

The storyboard that the task force creates shows a picture of an unhappy customer who had prior experiences with slow response time from prior complaints. The customer now has a billing problem and decides to try the new Web site. The customer logs onto the Web site and goes through security before accessing her account information. She is then able to retrieve her latest bill, highlight the erroneous charge, and request its removal from her bill. The system automatically routes the request to a customer service representative who researches the item and is able to access all necessary internal systems. The request is routed to an accounting person for final approval, and the error is corrected in approximately two hours. A confirmation of the correction is sent immediately after correction to the customer via e-mail. The next time the customer checks her e-mail she sees the correction, and the storyboard ends with the happy customer who buys more merchandise.

Now that a big picture of the business improvement is recorded and all participants agree on the action to further the development of the strategic idea, the task force begins to build the value circle for the whole initiative. They prioritize the list of business opportunities and highlight the top three ideas to increase business value from the storyboard. This process is repeated for identifying the top three risks and how they affect the business as well. The finance team presents alternatives for defining the survival line. All agree to use time, accuracy, and customer satisfaction retention as the metrics that will evaluate the business value of the initiative. Organizational issues relating to the need for service and sales to communicate more effectively and to develop improved communication skills with customers are identified as well.

The top business opportunity identified in the value circle is to provide self-service complaint tracking to customers through the Web, which will reduce response time significantly. A second opportunity is to provide a value-added fee-based service to generate additional revenues for the company. Risks associated with improving customer complaint tracking are that the current disconnected systems will continue to limit the level of benefits to customers, that customers would remain unsatisfied despite the changes that have been made, and that customers will not pay additional fees for increased personal services.

Limiting the opportunities and risks to only three ideas in priority order, as in Figure 7.2, helps the team and decision makers recognize that staff will have the capacity to complete only one to three key actions to support the initiative. This short-list approach encourages rigorous discussion and decision making from the outset of any initiative to derive business benefits.

There is still much debate about the value potential of this initiative. The group decides that tangible measures of customer loyalty and behavior, from error identification to customer notification, must be measured. Based on the customer survey, it appears that customers will wait only 24 hours for a status update on their complaints; the survival line must include this time parameter. Research reveals that the current customer response time is days instead of hours. Group members agree that this level of service is unacceptable and will force customers to go to competitors. At this point, only the criteria for decisions are determined because further investigation and consultation with others must occur.

Figure 7.2
Customer Service Initiative Value Circle

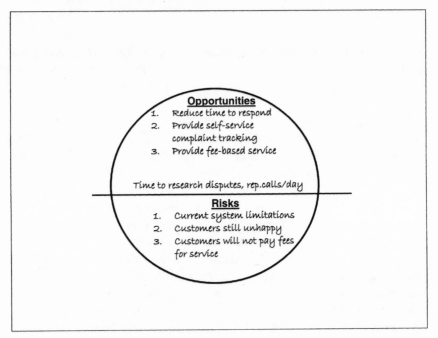

Printed with the permission of Project Concepts, Inc.

The group is not ready to calculate an actual breakeven point or other financial and service ratios for this effort at this time. Metrics and measures will be an important element used later in determining the initiative's survival when compared to other initiatives and investments.

Results of the working session are summarized for key managers and the call center vice president. The analysis of the customer experience indicates that rapid response time to customers means researching and correcting customer accounts within 24 hours. For this change to occur, productivity of the staff researching customer complaints must be increased. Web technology may be the best option for lowering the cost of responding to customer complaints. The priorities for the inquiry and concept generation are summarized in Figure 7.3.

The task force knows it is important not to totally eliminate ideas at this time because further development of the concept could indicate that these ideas should be revisited. The value circle becomes the value proposition statement used in making focused recommendations to executives for approval to establish and fund specific projects.

Figure 7.3
Initial Formation of the Seeing Solutions Map

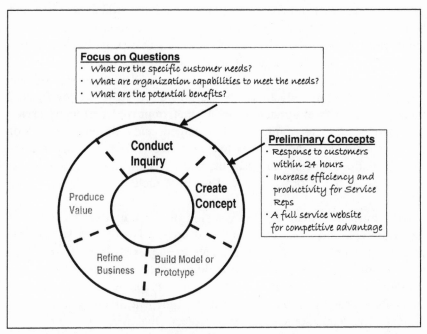

Printed with the permission of Project Concepts, Inc.

Bill Jones, the operations executive vice president, holds an initiative review meeting and introduces new information. He says, "According to the latest economic and marketing analysis, the company has decided to increase distribution of products through the Web. The marketing division is anticipating a three percent increase in sales. However, there is some concern that complaints may also increase. Marketing wants the task force to see what it can do to lower the rate of incoming complaints from all sources of distribution."

The review meeting continues with discussion of all the available information the task force has gathered and Bill decides that the opportunities and risks in the value proposition statement are even more compelling. They identify the highest priority opportunity as the one providing self-service complaint tracking to customers, which should reduce costs of complaint management by 20 percent. The task force must determine whether customer retention and revenue can be increased. Everyone agrees that the survival line for service improvement will be to resolve 90 percent of all complaints within 24 hours. The task force asks Bill to arrange for resources from marketing to finalize the potential for increasing revenue. Bill agrees and asks the teams to come back in two weeks with all relevant information to support a go/no-go decision.

The technology team contacts vendors, conducts product reviews, and holds preliminary design sessions. A prototype demonstrating the user interface for linking the Web site to the legacy system is developed. The business team updates the storyboards to illustrate the interaction between technology, service staff, and customers. These storyboards are reviewed with marketing to verify the effects on customer loyalty and revenue. The marketing staff estimate that improved customer service will increase the retention rate by five percent and will improve sales of additional products and services by two percent. With this specific information, the financial team uses the value proposition statement as the starting point for a formal financial analysis including intangible value criteria.

All teams now share the same vision of the initiative, its potential opportunities, and risks. One proposed project is to purchase and implement a Web-based, add-on product to the existing customer relationship management system, with high functionality in service and complaint management. A parallel technology project to integrate the customer management database with fulfillment technology is also important. The team defines business projects that will redesign service policies, processes, and procedures. Development programs for management and staff in sales and service are also proposed to optimize the use of the database, streamline reports, and improve analysis of complaint resolution and customer behavior. The teams recognize that significant staff retraining and data management standards are required to produce short- and long-term results.

A new version of the value proposition, Figure 7.4, is used to present the recommendations for specific projects to be approved at the next executive review. The updated value circle recommends the number one business opportunity as a self-service, Web-based complaint-tracking application that can be easily integrated with the existing customer relationship management system. The number two opportunity is to increase customer retention and increase sales over time. This option is considered to be much more realistic than trying to add fees for personalized service. If customer retention can be increased, then offering other related products and services, through the primary customer relationship management system, should generate additional sales. The risks of the improvements are that they would not meet overall customer expectations and that improving security and data management across multiple systems could increase costs. The survival line will use service metrics for response time, customer retention, and cross-selling to manage the business results.

Bill is impressed with the thoroughness and creativity, and he approves the projects that support the enhanced customer service initiative. He establishes the quarterly review schedule for initiative oversight and business-issue resolution. In addition, he requires all teams to meet at least monthly to coordinate efforts and resolve issues, and he wants them to use the company's formal project management processes.

Initiative Prototype and Refinement

Bill and his managers understand that the Seeing Solutions Map is still necessary and that the task force must work together to understand how the business will operate in the future to deliver measurable benefits. Task force and team members shift to the next regions of the Seeing Solutions Map, which pertain to projects. The two regions of the map that now should be considered are Build Model or Prototype and Refine Business, Figure 7.5.

Figure 7.4
Customer Service Initiative Recommended Value Circle

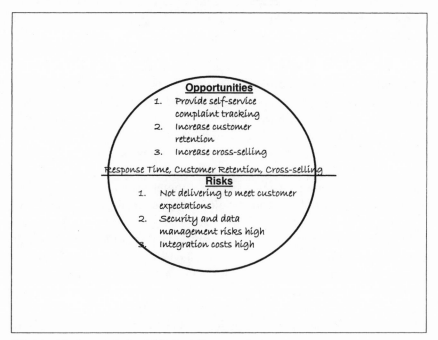

Printed with the permission of Project Concepts, Inc.

Figure 7.5
Service Initiative Prototype and Refinement

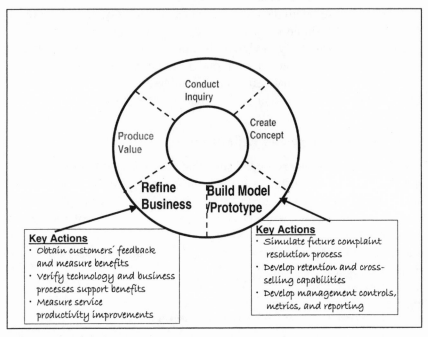

Printed with the permission of Project Concepts, Inc.

Prototype, in this context, means modeling or simulating how the business will actually operate with new technology, processes, and updated staff skills. The number one priority now of the task force is to begin simulating the new business environment that will manage customer complaints. The simulations are based on learning about the customer relationship management and database technologies. Business policies and processes are developed in a parallel effort with the technology investigation. Simulations using specific customer situations are run to validate that the technology and detailed tasks work together well. Staff performance and training needs are identified.

Marketing has arranged for a select group of customers to participate in alpha and beta tests to get the most value from the refinement region of activities. During the alpha testing, customers spot not only errors in the system but misleading or vague language on the Web site in communications that would generate the most complaints, frustration, and dissatisfaction. From this information, corrections are made rapidly to the Web site. The beta test indicates that customer satisfaction is very positive. Customers have even asked for self-service transaction tracking. In addition, selected business managers are finalizing the operating standards, communication, and evaluation processes. Logistics and fulfillment are tested to confirm that correction of complaints and updated orders can be completed well within 24 hours.

Bill has scheduled an initiative review meeting with the task force and the project teams in the last stages of completing the projects. They indicate that the customer relationship management system is being tested by sales and service and that appropriate training is in progress. All attendees are confident that customers will respond favorably to the new improvements.

IT tracks system performance, does a survey of customer usage for the relationship management system, and also identifies changes for the database now that it is integrated with the fulfillment system. Statistics are shared with business management and a plan is developed to correct errors in system usage and any delays in customer response time over 24 hours. The technology systems are refined as the business procedures are fine-tuned.

Produce Value

Bill understands that the next region of the Seeing Solutions Map should now be used to establish priorities for deriving business results from the completed initiative. He requires managers from all business units to report monthly measures of customer service improvement and sales trends. Bill knows it will take six months to a year for staff and managers to fully measure improvements and validate that the new business processes are strengthening relationships with customers. Necessary business reporting and analysis processes for management use are built and fine-tuned using real business situations in the Refine Business region. Managers will test the system by resolving sample complaints using the new technology. They will then review the proposed summary reports. Analysis of the reports should indicate whether response time to customers was improved significantly. Other information from staff is used for managers to improve controls and optimize use of the new technology. Key learning and tools developed from the completed projects are made available to business managers to continue deriving benefits from the technology.

The completed map prepared for the postimplementation review, shown in Figure 7.6, provides a comprehensive visual summary for Bill to communicate the priorities that drove the customer service initiative.

In the review, he points out the critical priorities used by the task force as the initiative progressed from formation to producing value. He highlights the importance of the value circle in helping the staff who are working on the individual related projects to maintain a clear focus on the desired business results and benefits. He shares with his fellow executives the importance of modifying priorities and revisiting early assumptions to further refine the business opportunities derived from the initiative. Bill sets the standards to track all customer complaints and to analyze those that take longer than 24 hours to resolve. New metrics and measures for customer satisfaction, tracking of retention, and cross-selling are being used and improvements are being made. Bill requires managers and staff to use the technology and related business process accurately and efficiently. He also assigns staff to explore functionality not currently in use in the newly implemented technology to identify future improvements in customer experience and business performance.

Figure 7.6
Completed Seeing Solutions Map for Service Initiative

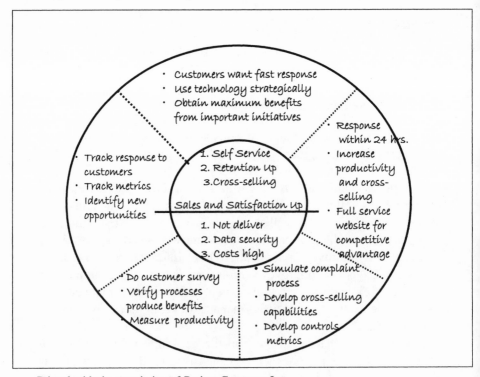

Printed with the permission of Project Concepts, Inc.

Finally, analysis and insights learned in this initiative are documented and recommended practices shared across the company for future technology and business performance improvement initiatives.

SUCCESSFULLY USING THE SEEING SOLUTIONS MAP

This case applied the entire Seeing Solutions Map to a business initiative, from the situation triggering action to completion and recognition of improved business results. Introducing the Seeing Solutions Map into a company takes a thorough understanding of the current company situation and the improvements that must be made as well as a clear commitment to follow through until positive results are achieved.

When introducing the Seeing Solutions Map into an organization, it is advisable to conduct an assessment of management experience and practices with technology prior to a technology initiative being launched. The assessment identifies ways to introduce the map that support organization strategy, strengths of the company, and high-priority needs for improvement to existing organization-wide patterns of action. An assessment also assists in identifying a basic business language and ways to integrate the map application with existing management practices. The goal is to identify how the map can be incorporated into the way mangers work and how it can add value quickly.

Additional key steps are to provide executive oversight for the Seeing Solutions Map discipline. After the assessment, the business issues and opportunities that are most appropriate for running a pilot of the map are identified. Once the pilot is conducted and the company has experience with the tool, executives can prioritize how to transfer the tool across the organization based on organizational needs and urgency.

Our experience introducing the Seeing Solutions Maps, reveals that staff who have not worked cross-functionally may need assistance with developing the skills and capabilities required to collaborate effectively and to understand the concepts associated with this new way of viewing initiatives. When staff experience how this tool helps them deliver business benefits and manage their work efforts more efficiently, they will apply the methods more consistently. The map provides a way for managers to become more effective in working with technology staff to achieve a clear business result.

A critical step for executives and the task force is to agree on evaluation criteria and potential metrics to evaluate how well the completed initiative performed before a formal post implementation review. Examples of evaluation criteria and metrics are:

- Post implementation, customer satisfaction equaled or bettered the standard 97 percent satisfaction level.
- Post implementation transaction accuracy increased 3 percent. Every percentage improvement reduces staff overtime by $10 thousand per month.
- Eight percent of all projects were completed and were within plus or minus 10 percent of the original estimated budget, schedule, and scope statement.

Executives and staff have a greater level of confidence in the benefits they obtain from technology investments when they have played a role in setting the objectives and contributed to achieving them. They know when investments meet or have exceeded specific business goals and when the company must improve processes, methods, and staff skills to deliver as needed on larger and more complex initiatives.

SUMMARY

The Seeing Solutions Map is designed to assist management in executing technology initiatives for business results. The tool also provides guidelines to executive management in oversight of technology initiatives to ensure that they are linked to strategy, linked to business objectives, and produce measurable business value. Using the thinking and action patterns the map outlines increases business benefits. It is time to make this kind of thinking and action a resource for all investments in technology. For the Seeing Solutions Map to be successful, executives must support bottom-up participation in strategic thinking and action and conduct initiative management reviews.

Chapter 9, Overseeing Initiatives to Generate Business Value from Technology, introduces a new way for executives to structure their oversight and decision-making processes for technology initiatives to achieve business value on a company-wide basis. The Seeing Solutions Map, in conjunction with strategic initiative management, and Chapter 8, Identifying the Value of Technology, gives executives new ways to identify and measure the success of critical technology that supports strategic business initiatives. The processes outlined in these two chapters provide the guidelines that companies need to obtain measurable business benefits from technology investments.

QUESTIONS FOR REFLECTION AND DISCUSSION

1. What processes and tools do managers use to achieve business objectives from technology investments?

2. When strategic ideas are generated, how do managers identify and document the opportunities, risks, and benefits for use by initiative teams and executives?

3. What methods do your managers use to approve initiatives and projects or to acquire products and services?

4. What methods do managers and staff use to identify and evaluate the anticipated business results while initiatives are in progress?

5. What guidelines do executives use in oversight of technology initiatives to ensure that they are linked to strategic business objectives and that they will produce measurable business value?

NOTES

1. Crane, D. B. "Seeing Solutions: Integrating Business, People and Technology to Generate Value." Workbook for graduate students by Project Concepts, Inc. Hayward, CA, 2000.

2. Crane, D.B. "Methodology and Revolutionary Projects" Paper presented at the Project Management Institute's 27th Annual Seminar/Symposium, Pittsburgh, 7–9 October 1996.

Chapter 8

IDENTIFYING THE VALUE OF TECHNOLOGY

In Chapter 1, Debunking the "Promise of Technology," we discussed a research study that showed that only 25 percent of chief executive officers were satisfied with the business results they had derived from technology.[1] Even with this high rate of dissatisfaction, most organizations focus on measuring uptime for the technology itself and rarely evaluate actual usage by end users or customers. Even more compelling is that post implementation reviews are not usually performed, therefore there is often no proof of the technology's value or that staff are even using it. Post implementation reviews actually measure results and identify additional work that may be required. There is a perception that measurement and evaluation are too costly, are too difficult, or may be used punitively. Executives can use measurement and evaluation to increase the business results from technology.

To illustrate the high risk of making investments in technology with little measurement of results, we use the metaphor of a patient going into a hospital for surgery. After check-in, the nurse prepares him for surgery and checks his vital signs, such as blood pressure, pulse, and temperature. If all checks out well, he goes into the operating room and the surgeons constantly check vital signs using monitoring devices, and if any change occurs they modify or stop surgery immediately. When the operation is complete, he is moved into the recovery room where his vital signs are still monitored. He would never think of telling the doctors to turn off the monitoring machines because they are too expensive. This metaphor can be applied to technology investments. Not measuring the value of investments that potentially touch every aspect of the business is as senseless as the patient who tells the doctor to turn of machines that monitor his vital signs. We have often heard the saying, the operation was a success but the patient died. This can be applied to initiatives when technology is implemented, but it is not used and does not provide value. It is essential to have mechanisms in place to monitor the vital signs of technology initiatives.

In this chapter we present methods for evaluating and establishing useful measures to identify the business benefits from technology. We apply the technology assessment described in Chapter 3, Realizing the Strategic Value of Technology, to illustrate how measurement starts when ideas about technology and business value begin to take shape. We will describe practical ways to evaluate and measure customer use and satisfaction with technology and highlight the importance of evaluating and measuring business readiness for technology, including end-user adoption. We then describe how business information is the foundation for measurement. Companies must know how technology controls the mission-critical information of the company and how it can be used for operating purposes and summarized in financial statements. The general rule is to measure meaningful and relevant information with the easiest tools available.

START MEASURING VALUE FROM TECHNOLOGY IN THE INITIAL TECHNOLOGY ASSESSMENT

Measurement of business value from technology starts in the 10 steps of the technology assessment. The 10 steps of the assessment are repeated here with suggestions and alternatives for evaluating and measuring results.

Step 1: Set the Assessment Goals and Objectives.

Executives determine the purpose, scope, time frame, budget, and outcomes of the assessment. They also outline how and when action will be taken as a result of the final report recommendations.

At this point, executives specify business outcomes for the initiative and how they must be measured at completion. When executives consider a new technology initiative, goal statements should include the key measures that will show that the goals were achieved. This action makes measurement a part of everything that follows, focusing on delivering results and value to the business. For example, all new product development efforts must include an estimate of revenue to be generated after release, estimated gross margins, net present value, or other quantitative analysis to win approval. This is the foundation for measuring value and results later.

Step 2: Form the Assessment Task Force.

Executives identify the organizational representatives who conduct the assessment. This task force develops the plan for the assessment to meet the goals and objectives.

The business case and all quantitative analysis of the initiative must be shared with the task force. Executives must prevent situations where task force members never receive the measurement criteria associated with business objectives. As the task force develops the plans for the assessment, it will take steps to further develop detailed metrics and measures associated with business goals and objectives. Using product development, for example, the task force selects a primary goal for revenue such as, $1 million in revenue over the first 12 months, with a gross margin of 36 percent. Members of the task force from sales and marketing make a plan to investigate methods for measuring and tracking sales results. Task force members from operations also identify a metric to verify that the gross margin is consistent with cost ratios for the current fulfillment process.

Step 3: Assess Existing Technology Capabilities.

The task force conducts the actual research required for documenting existing capabilities to deliver to business goals and objectives. Task force members work with internal staff to identify business needs and existing technology opportunities.

The task force reviews current technologies to determine whether or not their existing performance and reliability meets business needs. Identifying and measuring how existing technology offers greater capability is what is new and important. The results could be that technology is underutilized and needs reconfiguration to provide additional benefits to the company. When companies downsize, having fewer staff can mean that technology use is reduced. Taking the time to identify additional capacity and capability for major technology investments can delay or even eliminate additional technology purchases. An example is a system where capacity seems to be at its limit; the reality may be that the data needs to be purged and the system reconfigured to optimize capacity. The assessment that usually occurs in this case is to measure how much space is left, not to assess how the system can be reconfigured to free up more space. Setting periodic metrics for reconfiguration can allow for better ongoing utilization of existing technology and may delay the acquisition of new technology.

Step 4: Identify the Needs for New Technology.

The research in the previous steps reveals to the task force the needs that existing technology cannot fill. This step further documents actual business requirements. This documentation identifies what additional functionality is needed and leads to investigation of new technology.

Identifying business needs for technology requires information about current customer behavior and company marketing and positioning strategies. General demographic trends must be further researched to develop specific recommendations for new products, service improvements, and relationship management strategies to improve business performance. In addition, business processes, staff productivity, and information needs must be examined. If information regarding these is not readily available, executives must make a decision to obtain it to support the technology assessment. Recommendations for new productivity systems must be supported by operational statistics and financial analysis. As the company develops new strategies and objectives, each must be evaluated for the technology and business process support required to deliver the estimated benefits.

Step 5: Executives Set Business Priorities for Technology.

Executives now set priorities for technology to exploit existing systems to their greatest capability. They allocate budget to acquire new technology, which should reflect business needs, priorities, and measurements to prove their effectiveness. When these measures are in place, it is easier for executives to establish priorities for technology and to be able to understand the business results from changing priorities. The rate of change in priorities has a direct effect on the business outcomes of technology initiatives. Executives can track changes in priorities and business results achieved to determine whether decision patterns are supporting the desired outcomes.

Step 6: Assess Organizational Readiness.

The task force then assesses organizational readiness, staff use of technology, and customer attitudes. The assessment documents staff needs and concerns and identifies risks related to business performance and the total customer experience. The assessment also identifies all implications of technology change on organizational structure, business processes, policies, and management.

Measuring business readiness requires extensive data, analysis, and interpretation from all parts of the business. To do this effectively, detailed operations and customer information are required. Analysis tools such as business process mapping, statistical charts, and other methods from operations management aid in this effort. In addition, information on actual staff use of technology in performing detailed work tasks can be critical. The budget and resources for conducting a comprehensive business readiness assessment can be optimized in an organization-wide analysis. As individual initiatives are identified, the business readiness assessment further identifies specific business needs and organizational changes required. Business readiness assessments and measurement are not difficult but do require planning, efficient execution, and training of staff in use of appropriate tools. An analysis of business opportunities and risks is conducted to determine final priorities and budget approval.

Step 7: Set Business Priorities for Process Improvement and Organizational Change.

Executives use input from both assessments and business processes to determine what priorities are needed for organization structure, policies, and management. Executives have to identify the most critical organizational changes necessary to derive business benefit from the high-priority technology opportunities that support business objectives.

Business readiness is one of the most critical steps that can be made to ensure that technology investments deliver expected results and value. Understanding how processes that drive the business need to be either improved or changed as new technology is introduced is critical to the success of the new technology. In many cases organizational changes are necessary to deliver results from technology. Business readiness and change management are often overlooked. After the technology is implemented and operations are disrupted because of negative impacts to user productivity, management starts asking questions regarding stabilization. At this time, work might be disrupted as a result of staff dissatisfaction and employee backlash. This backlash can negatively affect business performance, cause legal implications, and ultimately mar a business's reputation. Positive and negative effects of change should be included in an initiative opportunity and risk evaluation.

Step 8: Conduct an Opportunity and Risk Evaluation of Technology Plans.

The task force conducts a comprehensive opportunity and risk evaluation to identify the potential benefits as well as the risks that might be gained or occur as a result of new technology. These opportunities and risks are then weighed to identify the highest benefit the technology can deliver and the most negative possible impact that might occur.

Use of quantitative risk management tools is recommended where risks and opportunities are identified and evaluated regarding their probability and potential impact for the company. When the opportunities are greater then the risks, little action may be needed. If the risks and opportunities are equal in weight or if risks are greater than opportunities, it is a signal that preventative actions are needed. These steps or precautions and the trigger that generates action should be measurable. An example is new technology to more effectively handle customer complaints. The business opportunity is high to make complaint resolution more efficient; the risks are also high that customers might not like the new system. The likelihood that the system can be more efficient is quantified as a probability of 90 percent, and the risk that customers might not like the new system is quantified as a probability of 80 percent. The quantified probabilities must be reassessed as the customer service initiative progresses. Actions to reconsider or stop work are identified at the formation of the initiative. Should the probability of customer dissatisfaction rise to 90 percent or more after preliminary system prototype reviews, the project should be reconsidered.

Changes in relative weights of risk versus opportunity can then be tracked over the course of an initiative. When risks significantly outweigh opportunities, this should be an indicator that the initiative should be modified or cancelled to reduce the risk. These risk evaluation tools translate management judgment about business risks versus opportunities into quantified weights.

Step 9: Prepare and Present Final Recommendations.

All prior information is combined into a findings and recommendations report. This report identifies the current business and technology capabilities and the future needs. It recommends how existing technology could be more fully utilized and new technology acquired to meet business and customer needs. The report also includes the findings and recommendations for organizational readiness and the effect of changes on business performance.

Step 10: Develop Business and Technology Roadmaps.

Roadmaps are developed by executives and are used after the assessment is conducted, findings are developed, and recommendations delivered. These maps support corporate initiatives and identify where existing and/or new technology can deliver strategic advantages. Scenarios are developed that exemplify how business and technology can be managed to provide business benefit.

In developing these scenarios, measurable benefits and decision criteria by initiative are necessary to know whether or not the scenarios meet company goals and objectives. After a scenario is chosen and implementation is complete, the actual results for each initiative are compared to the estimated benefits.

PRACTICAL MEASURES AND EVALUATION OF BUSINESS RESULTS FROM TECHNOLOGY

When the assessments are complete and metrics identified for every initiative, evaluating business results becomes easier. A common rule of thumb is that every initiative proposed should have one to three key metrics and/or measures that become the guideline for evaluating business results. When this rule is in place, organization-wide measurement can begin.

Make Measurement an Organization-Wide Process

Accountability for evaluating and measuring the value of technology should be organization-wide, as seen in Figure 8.1. Managers who have accountability for leading collaboration, making decisions, and implementing technology that affects the organization use these guidelines, verifying and delivering measurable benefits. Staff are responsible for gathering, analyzing, and interpreting measurable data to ensure that the benefits for organization-wide technology initiatives are achieved and risks reduced. Managers and staff who have local accountability for technology should also use the measurement guidelines to verify and deliver benefits within their business units and functions.

It can be a significant effort to implement organization-wide accountability metrics and measurement by initiative and project. The investment to build the measurement capability establishes a foundation for obtaining business value from technology. Staff must have the skills, methods, and tools to measure customer behavior and end-user interaction with technology. Management must have reporting tools to access and take action on this information daily, weekly, or monthly, as needed. The generation of useful information about business value from technology investments must be an ongoing effort.

Measure Customer Use and Satisfaction with Technology

The need to measure customer use and satisfaction with technology is often overlooked. Historically, companies have measured changes in sales volumes of new and modified products that are distributed and supported by technology. However, companies have not commonly in-

Figure 8.1
Organization-Wide Accountability for Evaluation and Measurement of Value from Technology

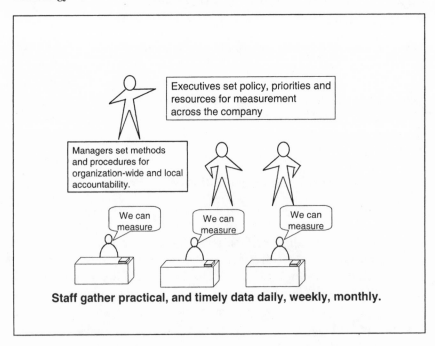

vested in observing and measuring the total customer experience or the value generated from technology and its effect on different customer segments. Many of the customer-focused methods for evaluating use of and satisfaction with technology are moving out of research and development and into product marketing and productivity improvement initiatives. Wherever the evaluation resides, there are tested methods that should be used to identify customer use, satisfaction with technology, and purchase decisions.

Observe Technology Use Where Buying Decisions Are Made

One way to observe how satisfied customers are with technology for purchasing goods and services is to view the sites where customers interact with the business through technology. In a bank, observe customers working with loan officers and administrative staff and using asynchronous transfer model (ATM) or other technology. If the company sells telecommunications products and services, it may even be necessary to go into homes to observe customers at work using technology. Observation can also be done through videotaping (with permission of the customer) to detect subtle details in use of technology. All of these observations are conducted by asking detailed questions and documenting the discussion. This information is very useful in fine-tuning the design of technology and product or service features to increase purchases and customer satisfaction.

Use Technology to Measure Customer Use and Satisfaction

Web technology and sophisticated databases now make it possible to gather detailed data on how customers interact with companies. An example of measuring business results from a new technology implementation is the case of a bank that invested in gathering customer information about the value of technology to secure relationships and improve access to products and services. The large bank was considering how to automate customer interaction and give customers access to the right departments quickly. The bank purchased interactive voice response technology that allowed customers to select the right department to meet their needs. In order to ensure that customers would accept the technology, the IT function conducted a pilot with a subset of bank customers. Staff measured the frequency with which certain departments were selected and identified how many levels of response customers would tolerate before they became frustrated. From this information they were able to develop the final selection options that met customer expectations. This was one of the first times that the IT function had used a detailed customer pilot and measured results. Through this process the bank was able to be the first in the market with this automated service capability and obtain positive public visibility. Staff continued to track customer hold duration and which departments received the most contacts. With this information the company adjusted call waiting times, staffing, and call routing. Now these interactive voice response systems are standard for many companies. Customers expect these options to be easy to use and not too cumbersome; they know when they reach a badly designed system. Metrics and measurement for interactive voice response systems are now very reliable and best practices for their use are well established.

Develop Technology and Business Staff to Gather, Analyze, and Interpret Information on Customer Use and Satisfaction with Technology

To ensure that measurement is in place, it is necessary to train staff to analyze customer needs and calculate business benefits from technology. Using training classes, workshops, and coaching, they learn to develop effective questions, conduct interviews, define measures of customer satisfaction, and propose excellent and valuable improvements in technology. When staff are trained to use these skills in a technology initiative, they are able to continue to improve the accuracy of estimates of benefits and identify and measure risks to retaining customers. This information is invaluable to the initiative and equips executives with vital information needed in making the toughest trade-offs as the completion date approaches.

Measuring and Evaluating Business Readiness

An entire section of the technology assessment is devoted to a business readiness assessment. Based on decades of work with organizations conducting business readiness assessments and supporting organization-wide programs, we have identified the important methods and tools that measure readiness. These methods include detailed observation, mapping how the organization works as a whole, and analysis of end users performing work in real business situations. This detailed information is necessary to identify when and where to measure.

The general rule is to go where the work is being done and get the best, in-depth information from the source. Review all available documentation on how work should be performed; observe how computers and other technology are used to complete the work. It is important to see how staff use technology as they are entering information to complete a customer order or to adjust an account. With this information it is possible to measure the average time and effort needed to accomplish a transaction or the likelihood of selling another product or service.

Create an Innovative Environment to Design Improved Business Processes

Encouraging staff to continually improve processes has been touted for years. Process improvement methods have been proven to be very effective in addressing business changes and supporting company growth. When staff and management are absorbed in keeping daily and monthly processes and procedures going without interruption, it is difficult to shift from this daily focus to new and innovative concepts of work. When staff are encouraged to participate in innovation, they can make important contributions because they know the current business and they also know where improvements can be made. Workshops where staff do creative exercises, make storyboards, and role-play new ways to do work are very effective. When staff participate in redesigning their work and even propose new processes, their commitment to the success of the initiative increases. The critical step after the creative efforts is to have staff identify metrics and measures to identify benefits and value of technology initiatives for customers, the company, and staff. These measures should be refined over the course of the initiative and used to evaluate results at completion.

Commit to Business Management and Staff Participation in the Technology Initiative

It is important to have business managers and staff involved from the outset of initiatives through their completion. Such involvement increases an initiative's success. In one case, a primary reason for failure of productivity improvement as a result of technology initiatives was that business staff involvement was low. Too often the initiative task force is composed of many technologists, a project manager, a business sponsor, and few business staff. This select group knows all the details of the technology and implementation plans, yet this information rarely reaches affected managers and staff. It is common that communication about the impending change is released shortly before implementation. This approach creates high risks for implementation and success.

One way to ensure success is by creating a collaboration and readiness map for the entire organization. It identifies not just the initiative task force but also all staff who must be involved in the planning of the initiative, in the selection of products and services, in the analysis and redesign of business processes, and in the testing and implementation processes. Collaboration and readiness ensure that appropriate management and staff give input to the task force, which results in better informed decisions. When the technology initiative reaches the completion stages, business staff are prepared with a readiness checklist to ensure that the new systems and procedures are implemented and stable. When the entire organization is informed and aware of the new technology, they can modify business processes and practices to reduce business risks and achieve measurable benefits.

Assess Training Needs for Management and Staff

It is important to assess the needs for end-user and management training when new technology is implemented. End users must be able to use the technology in a way that ensures that the work assignments are accurate, are complete, and meet deadlines to maintain customer relationships. Managers are frequently overlooked in the training assessment. They need training designed for their responsibilities if they are to maintain the stability of operations, service, and sales and to meet all contractual and service commitments to customers. Managers must understand how their staff will use the technology, the effects of technology on their staff's productivity, as well as the new reporting systems and analysis tools. Staff training on new technology and changes from current practices must be identified and appropriate training designed and delivered.

Model and Simulate Business Operations

When the risk of technology is identified, executives need to consider broader modeling or simulations of significant portions of the business. For businesses with high standards of quality and safety, such as aerospace, health services, or banking, a simulation of a full day's work volume or testing until accuracy and security of all transactions and information reaches 99 percent must be performed. The budget and resources to plan these complex and sometimes lengthy tests must not be overlooked. Metrics and measures for security and accuracy must be clearly identified.

Measure Organizational Change Management

Organizational change does not lend itself easily to measurement. A way to measure the effectiveness of change management for technology initiatives is to compare the results from different initiatives. The company can measure the staff acceptance and productivity results from initiatives that have used change management against those that have not. Based on the results of the evaluation, the company can determine what organizational change methods and approaches are producing measurable business value.

BUSINESS INFORMATION IS THE FOUNDATION OF MEASUREMENT

Quality and completeness of information across the organization are required if business value from technology is to be measured. The importance of quality information is more important than ever. Information itself is now being used as an indicator of investment quality. Standard and Poor's, the investment research company, conducted a study that showed that the amount of information companies provide in their annual statements can be directly correlated with their market risk.[2] The study found that companies that provide more complete information are lower risk for investors. A focus on improved business information and performance is an opportunity for executives to demonstrate rigor and discipline in all aspects of management. When companies can report measurable improvement in delivering value to customers with technology, investor confidence and competitiveness can be improved.

To ensure that business information is timely, complete, and accurate, it is essential to know how technology generates business information and how that information is compiled into financial reporting. A comprehensive analysis of technology controls, data integrity, and business use of information is necessary to verify the reliability of financial reporting. The analysis can be successful only when executives require all business units, functions, and support services to participate in the analysis with the goals of increasing benefits and reducing the risk from large and complex technology initiatives. In many cases the basic data to complete an organization-wide analysis can be gathered easily using existing technology tools.

An organization-wide analysis of technology systems, information, and financial reporting should be conducted with a team from accounting, process improvement, business operations, software development, and technology. Analysis and interpretation of the data must be performed by skilled staff who can critically examine the raw data and determine whether it accurately describes business transactions and use of financial accounts, and whether it will produce summary reporting that will meet regulatory requirements. In the analysis, financial transactions originating from operations should be traced through each software application and mission-critical business process. Figure 8.2 illustrates a high-level flowchart linking technology controls, business operating information, and financial reporting.

After operational and financial transaction details are charted, an evaluation can be conducted to determine if technology systems are using the appropriate business rules and controls to reduce errors in data interpretation. This evaluation should also include examination of detailed operating procedures to confirm whether staff use of information and technology is consistent with policy and controls.

If, as a result of the evaluation, inconsistencies and errors are found,

Figure 8.2
Financial Reporting of Business Operating Information and Technology Controls

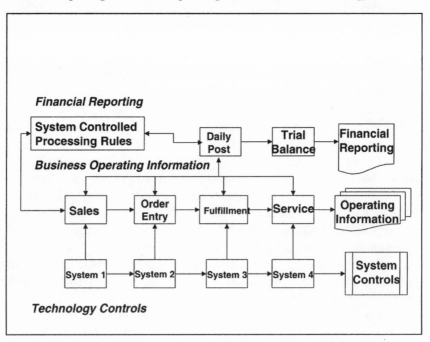

the task force then explores responses to key questions to identify recommendations for improvements. Sample questions might be:

- What are the highest priority improvements that must be made in information use and control?
- How will improved technological controls and business practices affect financial reporting?
- How will investors and regulators respond to and interpret changes in financial reporting?

After these questions are answered, business policies, standards, and detailed practices might need to be modified. The analysis team then defines and prioritizes recommendations for improvements in technology processing rules and controls, detailed staff procedures, changes to the chart of accounts, and summary reporting. Management can then determine the budget and resources to improve technology and business operations. Often many of the issues can be resolved quickly and at low cost. However, if the comprehensive information and reporting analysis has not been conducted for many years, then significant issues could surface that require corrective initiatives to be formed to solve them.

WHAT YOU CAN DO: SET A STARTING POINT FOR MEASUREMENT OF VALUE FROM TECHNOLOGY

Use the tools presented in this chapter to set a starting point for measuring the value from technology investments in your company. Steps for setting the baseline are:

- Identify the starting point and compare it to the expected measurable benefits.
- Identify the difference between expected and measurable benefits; ask questions to bridge the gap.
- Use the technology assessment to identify the highest priority measures of value.
- Ensure that a business readiness assessment is completed, and identify the measures necessary to safely control changes in operations and staff responsibilities.
- Analyze how existing and new information is controlled and managed across technology systems and business operations and how it is summarized in financial statements.

- Define the minimum standards for measuring benefits and value from technology at formation, in progress, and upon the completion of initiatives.

- Interpret and evaluate the measurement efforts to improve the oversight of technology initiatives in the future.

SUMMARY

Disclosure of more accurate and complete information is linked to actual business performance. Executives must use technology investments to respond to investor demands and manage the company-wide business drivers. Measurement and evaluation of the business value of technology investments is not done frequently over the duration and conclusion of initiatives; it will take time to change. The critical areas for measuring business value through technology are the effects on customer behavior, business readiness, and productivity. Organizations must begin to analyze and evaluate how information from technology systems affects business operations and financial reporting. Companies can no longer neglect measurement. Business survival depends on accurate, complete, and timely information. Knowing how technology supports business performance is vital.

QUESTIONS FOR REFLECTION AND DISCUSSION

1. How are metrics and measures for technology initiatives identified in assessments?

2. How are staff involved in measuring and evaluating the business value from technology?

3. How is customer information incorporated into technology initiatives?

4. How are estimated benefits validated and measured over the course of initiatives?

5. How are business readiness assessments conducted and the information used in technology initiatives?

6. How are staff trained to use customer-focused and operations productivity methods?

7. How does your company control and use information for financial reporting?

NOTES

1. Tallon, P., K. Kraemer, V. Gurbaxani. "Executives' Perceptions of the Business Value of Information Technology: A Process-Oriented Approach." *Journal of Management Information Systems* (Spring 2000): 145–174.

2. Beck, R. "Missing Info Linked to Poor Performance." *San Francisco Chronicle,* 16 October 2002, C3.

Chapter 9

OVERSEEING INITIATIVES TO GENERATE BUSINESS VALUE FROM TECHNOLOGY

Every year executives conduct their one- to three-year planning for major initiatives and objectives. Then they immediately ask their staff to identify, justify, and launch projects as soon as possible to achieve these initiatives and objectives. Even when there are successful processes in place, such as a business plan, we have found that after project approval, there is little connection back to the initiatives and objectives that generated them. Even when companies have monthly or quarterly business reviews, progress on strategic initiatives frequently wanes after a quarter or two. When technology projects are running, they drop off of executive and senior management radar screens because they are viewed as details to be managed by middle management and project managers. Typically little or no effort is made to evaluate the overall effects of all projects on business performance as it relates to achieving critical strategies. This lack of action leads to unfulfilled technology objectives that result in increased business risks, higher future operating costs, and weaker competitiveness in markets. It can also result in large technology investments, especially infrastructure, being under utilized strategically and failing to provide company-wide benefits.

In this chapter we propose that executives must be accountable for overseeing management processes for technology investments to ensure their positive effects on business performance. The detailed execution of technology projects remains with middle management. We call this executive oversight process *strategic initiative management*. This process fills the gap between business strategies, objectives, and initiatives and the projects they generate. Ignoring the gap keeps the company from tracking and evaluating these projects as they relate to productivity, customer relationships, and the realization of proposed business benefits. The strategic initiative management process ensures that technology infrastructure is managed as a strategic organization-wide asset and not as separate products and purchase agreements. It also allows investment opportunities and risks in initiatives to be identified before the initiatives generate actual projects.

The strategic initiative management process allows executives to manage technology to maximize business opportunity, mitigate risk, and manage the implications of technology for the business as a whole. The process focuses on revealing departures from standards and misuses of technology that affect the business. Oversights of the most critical issues that affect business performance should be managed from the outset, during, and after implementation of initiatives. Using this process gives executives the opportunity to see how separate projects relate to initiatives by illustrating their effect on financial information, operations, and management practices. The process reveals where a specific technology initiative or project has a much broader effect on the entire business than expected. Ineffective technology initiatives and bad technology implementations that involve financial transactions frequently negatively impact the financial position of the company. The strategic initiative management process is especially effective with large technology initiatives that affect the bottom line. Lastly, strategic initiative management allows executives to create formal company-wide policies to ensure that the value, risks, costs, and trade-offs found within major technology investments are managed from a strategic perspective.

Many of the current strategic planning methods focus on stating high-level strategies and objectives, but they do not require accountability for the results of projects. Strategic planning ranges from the very disciplined Hoshin planning to the method known as muddling through. In the Hoshin planning process objectives are derived from the top three corporate strategies, and projects are launched to meet these objectives. Experts in the Hoshin planning process acknowledge that there is a weakness in the deployment system because the connection between the means of accomplishing the objectives and its effect on strategy is not always clear.[1] They recommend filling the gap through cross-functional collaboration, management reviews, and performance planning, which is a good start but which does not go far enough. Using primarily individual performance plans cannot fill an organization-wide gap between strategies, initiatives, projects, and benefits to customers and the business.

For companies using strategic or business planning methods with less discipline than Hoshin methods, the transition from strategy to projects can be viewed as muddling through. By muddling through we mean that initiatives are announced, many projects are launched, and the connections to broader strategies are lost. This approach neglects the business target and leaves delivering results to stakeholder expectations and business value to chance. This method does not allow the company to measure the effectiveness of projects in terms of business performance. We have found that some companies have tried to better link business objectives to initiatives, but when they filter down to the project level the connection is lost. Formal oversight structures are a first step in connecting initiatives and objectives to projects.

CURRENT APPROACHES TO MANAGING INITIATIVES AND PROJECT PORTFOLIOS

Attempts to bridge the gap between initiatives and projects have been made by utilizing devices such as a project management office (PMO) and project portfolio management (PPM). They only focus on a part of the problem: managing approved and funded projects. The role of both a project management office and portfolio management is to ensure that projects stay on schedule, use standardized practices, and meet their budgets.

Neither PMO nor PPM fully addresses whether projects are designed to meet business needs, when to stop projects if they are not delivering value, or how completed projects actually deliver to initiatives and objectives. In many companies, research and analysis preceding project definition and funding are absorbed by the operating budget. In addition, projects are usually focused on implementation of technology itself and not on customer behavior or staff use. Frequently, expenses for staff efforts for business readiness and modification of processes and detailed procedures affected by technology are hidden in the operating salary budget and are never associated with the investment. Finally, after the decision is made to approve and fund a project, it is extremely difficult to stop it if conditions arise that make it no longer viable. A project completion mindset takes over or the desire not to be associated with a failed project prevents staff from raising issues or recommending that the project be stopped. Many times there is no way for staff to raise issues or for executive management to know that these situations occur. Companies can no longer be blind to this financial drain or the lack of results from technology investments.

Many companies use PMO for product development and technology acquisitions to better control related projects. PMO is very common in aerospace, manufacturing, and biotech, where interdependent projects are common. Both of these methods improve priority setting, scheduling, budgeting, and resource management. They centralize project information and focus on the details of each project.

Throughout the 1990s, the State of Washington was victim to a series of failed technology projects.[2] First, the COSMOS project was cancelled in 1989 after the state spent $20 million, and caseworkers found it easier to do the work manually. Then in 1990, the Department of Licensing embarked on a computer replacement project that was meant to be a $40 million project but after two years was $10 million over budget. Another project by the Department of Social and Health Services was to computerize nine years of its welfare records. In 1991, the Automated Client Eligibility System began and was put on hold a year later when cost estimates for initial work doubled. After five years, the system finally went online.

These failed technology investments were all authorized by the legislature but delivered little if any return and in most cases cost significantly more then the original approved budgets. This pattern was not uncommon for the state, and in 1999 legislators finally took action to eliminate this waste of state funds. They embarked on a new program of managing technology initiatives with a PMO structure. They identified all related projects and assessed which ones truly could deliver to objectives. Those that could not were cancelled or combined with others. The legislators viewed the criticality of the remaining projects, prioritized them, and decided how to allocate resources to the top ones in order to receive measurable results. This dramatic change took time, but the results that the technology delivered were impressive. After changing to a PMO, they found that their project success rate increased dramatically. This eliminated competing projects and allowed better visibility into the whole effort. The state gained more control over what it was spending money on, what standards were used to manage the projects, and what the projects could deliver. The legislature began to see positive results from the PMO and supported the move to this way of managing critical technology investments.

PMO and PPM are focused on assisting project managers in delivering project deliverables on time, budget, and within scope. Neither the PMO nor the PPM really guarantee that projects are tied to company objectives and strategic initiatives, because their primary goal is to complete projects and deliverables, not to ensure that strategies as a whole are accomplished. Project management methodology clearly defines projects as accountable for deliverables and management as accountable for defining strategic goals and getting business results. These methods do not include identifying the connection of one project to another and overall business performance. Therefore, companies can have an excellent product development and project management processes managed by PMO or PPM and yet still lose money or commit grave errors with customers and markets.

STRATEGIC INITIATIVE MANAGEMENT

We propose that a flexible, strategic initiative management process be used to fill the gaps in current methods to meet the demands of future business pressures and to seize opportunities from technology. Strategic initiative managementis a new way for management to interpret strategic information about technology investments before projects are defined, when they are in progress, and after implementation. It allows executives to understand how different projects and parts of the organization work together to generate value.

Figure 9.1 shows the strategic initiative management process flow. The far left column of the flow shows the normal executive decision process for translating strategies and initiatives into projects. It further highlights the development of a value proposition for each initiative as described in the Seeing Solutions Map.[3] The process flow illustrates how reporting on delivery of the value proposition is progressing. The periodic reporting and evaluation steps ensure that opportunities and risks are identified and actions taken to ensure that technology is utilized strategically for the benefit of customers and the company. Excessive risks can be identified early and minimized or adjustments can be made to initiatives and priorities. If external forces trigger reevaluation of the strategic direction, the strategic initiative management process can ensure rapid adjustment of the initiatives and projects themselves.

If one or more projects are launched to implement the technology initiative, then each of the projects must have a defined value proposition with similar prioritized information. The accountable executive ensures that the project value proposition statements support the higher-level initiative value proposition. As the projects are launched, the value propositions of all projects are cross-checked against other projects. Projects that are redundant, vague, or of minimal value can be identified and eliminated or modified to increase the value of the overall initiative. An additional advantage of this approach is that resources can be distributed

Figure 9.1
Strategic Initiative Management Process Flow

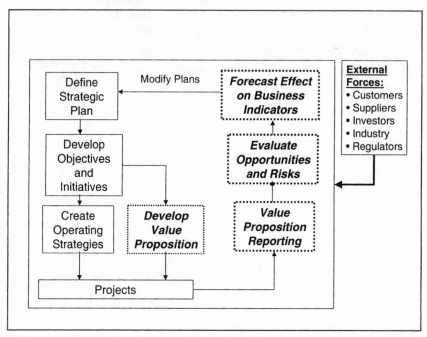

based on value criteria, rather than by forcing individual projects to compete against one another for resources when they really must work together.

The organization must make it a policy to require strategies, initiatives, and objectives be linked. As strategic technology initiatives are developed and objectives identified prior to funding, a core value proposition statement that includes the information presented in the value circle from the Seeing Solutions Map must be developed (see Figure 9.2). As described in Chapter 7, Establishing a Value-Driven Management Process for Technology, the value circle first lists the top three business opportunities in priority order. Then it states the key business drivers and initial breakeven points and the survival line of the initiative. Key business drivers can be per unit costs, cycle time to complete a business process, or a vital business-operating ratio such as revenue per employee. Finally, the three highest risks to achieving the initiative are listed in priority order. The business drivers and breakeven points can immediately become the business criteria for evaluating the actual business results and value the initiative contributes to achieving the strategic objective. The executive accountable for obtaining the business results from the technology initiative approves the value circle and imposes it as a guide for future projects and work efforts.

Executives are accountable for ensuring that the initiative's focus on realizing value from technology investments continues as projects move through the implementation life cycle. Monthly or quarterly business reviews led by executives are essential to resolve the highest-priority issues about trade-offs on value among initiatives and projects from a strategic perspective. The purpose of the reviews is to track, compare, and evaluate whether the value proposition statements from projects still support the objectives and estimated benefits of the initiative. Project management criteria (schedule, cost, and scope) are one source of data for understanding the value of projects. Issues and risks due to dependencies between technology initiatives and projects should also be iden-

Figure 9.2
Linking Initiative and Project Value Propositions

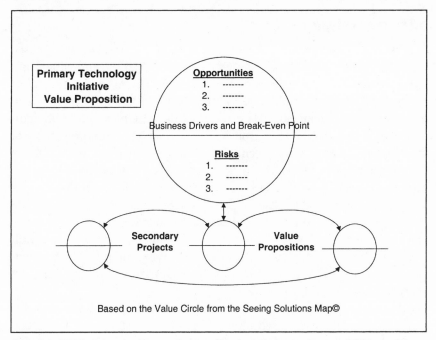

Copyright 2002. Printed with permission of Project Concepts, Inc., and Margery Mayer.

tified to understand their effect on value. Strategic initiative management gives a view of how the total technology infrastructure is being fully leveraged for value by all initiatives.

Utilizing an ongoing method to ensure that new initiatives are linked and benefits are achieved is vital in today's fast-paced, demanding business environment. From our experience, strategic initiative management ensures that the executive level addresses opportunities and risks concerning the delivery of value from technology when it is critical to business performance. In addition, middle management sponsors and project teams obtain clearer direction on how to focus project outcomes to achieve specific benefits to customers and internal staff. This is an important improvement over implementing technology merely to meet a deadline.

Applying Strategic Initiative Management

The value of applying strategic initiative management can be illustrated by applying it after the fact to the examples from Chapter 2, Understanding the Victim's View of Technology.

The User's Won't Use It!

This case was about a hospital that wanted to provide a Web-based system to automate staff recruitment, fill many open positions, and improve patient care. Executives emphasized that they must do this project to keep the hospital competitive. Staff were not asked to identify potential risks to the organization as a result of the new technology. In addition, they were discouraged from raising issues or identifying risks of the project. When the new technology was implemented, the staff, not feeling their concerns had been heard, did not want to use it. The executives did not know this and waited for the personnel recruitment system to produce better results. Improved results never materialized because the system was underutilized and undervalued by staff. Blame ran rampant as IT blamed the executives for not supporting the technology and staff blamed executives for not involving them in the decision-making process. The final result was that the improved patient care that everyone hoped for did not occur.

Let's take a look at this case with the application of strategic initiative management. The Web-based initiative to improve staff recruitment and patient care is proposed and approved. The project is now called "The Right Staff for the Right Care." This technology initiative identifies appropriate projects to ensure that the strategic objectives of the hospital are achieved. A sponsoring executive is assigned to this initiative until it is completed and results are evaluated. The executive calls a working meeting with the key senior managers who together develop a value proposition statement for the initiative. Next, the group identifies all the projects needed to support the initiative objectives and deliver on the value proposition.

Figure 9.3 shows how strategic initiative management works for this company. The major initiative of faster hiring of more experienced staff is linked to the initiative objective of improving patient care. Pressure from competitors and expectations from the marketplace make this initiative vital to continue and increase the business. The initiative identifies three projects that will support the effort. They are Website development, recruitment effectiveness, and patient care. These projects have the following goals:

- Website development.This technology project would capture all resumes through direct entry by applicants or scanning of paper resumes

Figure 9.3
Value Proposition Integration for Web Initiative

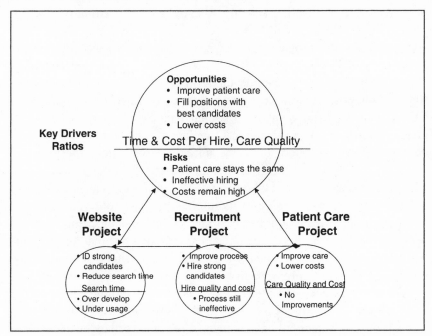

by staff. The system would also match the best-qualified applicants to the open positions.

- Recruitment effectiveness. Recruiters would use key words to search for the best candidates for open positions. The overall time from application receipt to start on the job would be reduced.

- Patient care. By filling open positions with well-qualified candidates and bringing them up to full capability quickly, patient care would be improved

The value proposition for the initiative is the large circle on the upper portion of the diagram. Business opportunities of initiatives are listed in priority order. Key drivers or ratios the initiative will affect are identified as time, cost, and quality. Risks involved in the initiative are then listed on the bottom of each circle in order of significance. The risks are prioritized based on initial management judgment and are to be validated as the initiative progresses. Using this framework, executives have a clearly documented way to communicate the vital elements of the initiative that must be delivered to create value.

Each project then defines a value proposition statement to specify how it will support realizing the initiative goals. The Website development project's value proposition statement begins with the listing of key opportunities in priority order. Key drivers of time, cost, and quality remain constant. Now the project manager has a clear statement to guide the effort directly linked to the initiative. The value proposition statement for the Web project is to identify the right candidate with the right skills for the right cost. Recruitment and patient care projects now build their value proposition statements in a similar manner. Similarity of the language and format allow the projects to relate to each other to collectively deliver the desired outcomes to the initiative level. Since the projects' staffs are able to communicate clearly and efficiently about opportunities, risks, and issues, the overall risks of the projects and the initiative are reduced. The estimated value of the initiative is also more reliable.

These projects are now reflected in the overall strategic initiative and periodic reporting process. The executive may now use parts of the initiative value proposition statement as evaluation criteria to review the progress of the three projects. In reviews, discussion does not focus on the details of project execution but on issues concerning realizing the opportunities and ultimate benefits to the company. The executive informs project managers of any changes in priorities or key business drivers that affect their projects. Project managers are able to inform the executive of risks and issues that could negatively affect the outcome of a project or the overall initiative.

As strategic initiative management progresses, the key drivers, operating metrics, and performance requirements for the future patient care environment are refined. Staff adjust their procedures, practices, and performance evaluation criteria to meet the new way of working and improving the patient care environment. The new operating standards and metrics continue to be used and improved over time. In the next executive review, staff will report on the completion of the projects, results achieved, and lessons learned.

Where's the Software?

Let's see how strategic initiative management affects the actions among executives in another story from Chapter 2, Understanding the Victim's View of Technology. In this case a service provider hires an outside software development company to build a new, robust database engine for its client policy reporting system. Benefits from this initiative are promised to customers, and competitors already have this new functionality. The executive who makes the decision to select the vendor does not ask for an internal risk analysis of the current situation. When the vendor requests significant additional funds to complete the work, he accepts the developer's statement and continues until the next crisis arises.

With a strategic initiative management process in place the new database engine is approved because of its competitive importance. A value proposition statement is developed immediately and used to evaluate the project at executive reviews on at least a quarterly basis. When after the first three months of the project a request comes in for additional funding, a red flag is immediately raised. All of the executives have to examine the project to evaluate the risks in relationship to realizing benefits. The high-risk level leads an executive with a focus on value to consider a new go/no-go decision on the project. He stops the project and asks questions about the vendor's capability to deliver the system. The executive realizes he cannot afford to continue this effort without considering other alternatives. A reasonable alternative is identified and justified, and the project is restarted with changed expectations. This approach reduces expenditures on wasted effort. Selecting a more productive vendor brings this project back on track, reduces overall costs, and delivers a high-quality product, allowing the company to become more competitive.

Both of the projects discussed highlight how strategic initiative management can allow executives to see issues and risks associated with initiatives early enough to take appropriate action. There are triggers in place that identify potential risks when action should take place. Strategic initiative management is a process that ensures that executives know critical issues early, have a mechanism for action, and can better maximize their technology investments for company and customer value.

Applying Strategic Initiative Management to the Pace of Technology Innovation

The rapid pace of change and the importance of the capital budget dedicated to technology investments are forcing executives to be more accountable for managing opportunities and risks associated with these investments. Along with managing the economic purpose, organization structure, policy, operations, and financial performance, executives now have to manage the direct and indirect effects of technology. It is no longer enough to develop and maintain the right products, services, and support systems. Executives must understand that technology affects how the entire company works for the benefit of customers. Technology can make or break customer loyalty by how easily customers interact with it. In addition, the company must continue to attract investors, deliver increased shareholder value, and maintain trust with accurate, timely information. To balance all of these competing interests, executives must know the role of technology as it supports their business and decisions.

Strategic initiative management helps executives see and manage the company-wide effect of technology on an ongoing basis—not just at funding decision points. The shift to this more accountable viewpoint enables the executive to improve technology and business planning as an integrated activity. Executives can quickly make changes to minimize any negative business effects and better understand how technology generates value from a broader financial perspective.

The strategic initiative management process puts equal emphasis on risk management and raising issues as actively promoting and seeking opportunity. Managing growth with reasonable risk to stakeholders is now critical. Risk management needs to include a clear statement of the risk, an estimate of the probability it will occur, and a ranking of its significance in relationship to other risks. Risks have to be reviewed vis-à-vis the entire business environment and their long-term implications and effects on internal policies and actions.

One way of assessing implications that affect companies is through the process of determining risk and value. Figure 9.4 shows a way to evaluate risks in terms of their probability, impact on value, and significance to the business. If risks have both high probability and high impact, they should produce a high-priority effort to reexamine all initiatives and restructure the allocation of resources, priorities, and go/no-go decisions. The risk analysis must be reviewed and updated regularly as the initiative progresses. Frequently, as risks that have been rated as medium or even low are clarified, the probability that they will occur and the impact to the organization if they do occur, quickly becomes a critical risk to the business. A full risk analysis gives executives a way to clarify the reasonable expectation of success in the face of change.

Risk management logic may also be applied to company-wide technology investment needs. Think of strategic initiative management as a way to manage technology similar to an investment portfolio that requires longer-term management and decision making. Risk assessment was first introduced in Chapter 3, and now similar questions need to be asked, such as:

- What level of risk is the company willing to bear?
- Are limited resources increasing risk?
- How can limited resources be used wisely to achieve benefits and mitigate risks?
- Are schedules unrealistic? Are unrealistic schedules increasing risk for achieving results?

Figure 9.4
Evaluating Risk and Value

Risk	Probability of Occurring	Impact if Risk Occurs	Priority	Executive Action
1.				
2.				
3.				
High = H, Medium = M, Low = L				

- What conditions should trigger a change in the management of the initiatives?

- How does the company know whether or not the degree of risk has exceeded the opportunity and whether to discontinue the investment?

Updating the risk level of the technology investment is vital to understanding the potential benefits and value of the initiative while in progress. If the original business case estimated a 5 percent increase in revenue from a new fee service, and the probability of success is 75 percent, then the company should only expect a 3 to 4 percent increase in revenues as a result (see Figure 9.5). This calculation (multiply the expected increase by the probability of success) is a standard practice in estimating the effect of risk on benefits for projects. When the initiative is implemented and the actual fees paid by customers are examined, then the benefits can be fully understood.

Implementing Strategic Initiative Management

When introducing strategic initiative management into companies, due diligence in setting a foundation for success is essential. There must be careful examination of the history of similar efforts and of the funda-

Figure 9.5
Re-Evaluating Risk and Value

Risk	Probability of Occurring	Impact if Risk Occurs	Priority	Executive Action
1. Est. 5% revenue increase in error	H	H	H	Survey indicates sales increase is 3-4 percent. Action: Modify sales plan
2. Schedule change	L	M	M	
3. Fulfillment vendor not selected	M	M	M	
High = H, Medium = M, Low = L				

mental business purpose for making major change. Utilizing staff knowledge is essential to obtaining information on how best to introduce strategic initiative management for success. Staff know the current business and fully understand the substantial work effort and demands involved in introducing change through technology. Staff enthusiasm at launch will quickly translate into hard work and resolution of difficult issues. We recommend that if the company is underperforming and must make changes to survive, the communication and rollout of the changes should be stated and opportunities and risks identified to all affected managers. If the company is doing very well, then staff need to understand the sources for growth and how they can best support opportunities. Elaborate efforts to mask problems and issues to push a new program often overwhelm and frustrate staff in understanding and acting on the vital business needs.

In other major organization-wide technology change initiatives, forming a task force or team of volunteers who want to participate in making the company more successful is vital. These individuals are usually very loyal and come from all levels of the company. The volunteer team conducts a readiness assessment for the change. This assessment identifies existing processes, technology support systems, and parts of the organization most or least likely to utilize the new approach effectively. The team works with one executive who obtains support from the whole executive team in managing technology as a strategic asset to the company. This executive sponsor assists in defining how, when, and where to position the process change. Executive sponsorship is essential to ensuring that the new process is utilized at all levels.

It is important to obtain this high level of executive and staff commitment so that technology is successful. In some situations we have seen low commitment by the chief executive officer to any new process or major change. If an executive sponsor is not in place, it will be very difficult to roll out an initiative and get agreement from staff at all levels. If staff recognize that the whole executive team is committed to the success of the effort, then they focus their efforts on making the change relevant and successful.

The company must design the strategic initiative process to match its distinct business needs and opportunities. For strategic initiative management to fit efficiently with how executives oversee company performance, one option is for technology initiatives to be linked to the periodic evaluations of business performance. Executives expect to report every month or at least quarterly to the chief executive officer on how their divisions, profit centers, or functions support business objectives.

Executives should be required to include in their reports how the high priority technology initiatives that they are accountable for are being managed to deliver specific benefits at a manageable risk.

Strategic Initiative Management in Action

The strategic initiative management process in action can be best illustrated by a hypothetical company situation. Let's use JIT Incorporated, a just-in-time manufacturing company, and address its need for lowering inventory costs. JIT has warehouses on the East and West Coast with too much inventory. Their competitors have already moved to just-in-time inventory management and have significantly reduced costs. JIT, as it name states, has to move to just-in-time inventory management in order to stay competitive.

The executive vice president of operations, Joe Black, is charged with executing this critical initiative. He was successful in implementing an enterprise-wide technology solution for another company and was recruited by JIT to do the same for them. Joe wants to use a strategic initiative management process; because of his prior success, he sees the benefits of managing critical technology initiatives this way. His prior implementation was successful by project management standards, but he knew the business could have derived more value if it had used strategic initiative management.

The first thing Joe does is to make the JIT inventory management effort a critical initiative. He identifies the key business drivers that will benefit from this initiative, such as a two-day order to delivery. Joe assesses the potential magnitude of the effort and clarifies his role in obtaining resources and support from his peers. With this support he can ask for volunteers across the company who can make the initiative and its projects successful. Joe knows he has to understand the total costs and the total effort to deliver the value from this initiative.

The volunteer task force assesses the readiness of the business and technology to achieve just-in-time inventory and improve competitiveness. They report their findings and propose technology and business projects to address readiness needs, technology requirements, and business process improvement. The projects are identified and initiative budgets estimated.

The two technology projects identified are upgrading the existing inventory management system and developing a supply chain capability that would include distribution and logistics. Both of these must be integrated with each other as well as with legacy financial accounting and reporting systems to be successful. The business work efforts required to ensure that business readiness is complete include an organization-wide policy and structure update, a process change for delivering just-in-time inventory management, improved use of the existing data warehouse, new inventory management alternatives, and personnel position changes. The estimated budget for the technology projects is $10 million. The estimate for the business readiness project is about $3 million. This budget projection covers a multiyear effort. The relationships among the value proposition statements for the initiative and the three projects are illustrated in Figure 9.6.

When the financial projections are completed, the team comes back together with Joe to evaluate the risk and opportunities for each project, across projects, and for the overall initiative. The levels of risk and opportunities are grouped by priority and value to the company. From this work, the roadmap for the multiyear initiative can be developed with a combination of project and business value criteria. Joe and the task force team recognize that this is a new way of thinking and acting for the

Figure 9.6
Value Proposition Integration for JIT Inventory

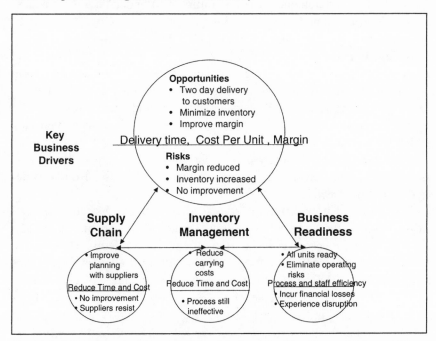

organization but potentially very effective in value. From this point the specific projects are approved and funded and formally tracked through the company project management process. Joe manages the progress on the overall delivery of business value from the projects in periodic strategic initiative management reviews.

WHAT'S DIFFERENT ABOUT STRATEGIC INITIATIVE MANAGEMENT?

Introducing the concept of a value proposition for a technology initiative is rather revolutionary in practice. When we have introduced this concept into discussions with executives and leaders for large technology initiatives, the individuals are surprised to be asked to state, evaluate, and prioritize the value proposition of the whole initiative and individual projects. Up to that point they have usually focused on just the technology purchase or implementation itself. When they start discussing the opportunities and business drivers for the initiative, the discussion is very lively and at times exciting. Participants in the discussion realize that the choice of technology and how it is implemented in the organization affects specific operating and financial ratios as well as specific line items on the financial statements. The commitment to understand the business results from technology rises in priority.

Sometimes the discussion of risks is very difficult. Many organizations have developed an environment where open discussion of challenges and risks is subtly avoided. To raise too many issues is considered bad form or career limiting. We have to reverse this conditioning to help managers and staff recognize that risk management is a fundamental factor in defining the measurable level of business results. When management and task forces understand that a complete picture of the potential business results of technology is really invaluable to the organization, then everyone can be mobilized to manage and execute the initiative from a value-generation perspective.

Discussion of how different projects affect one another and the business overall is also new to companies. Project managers are taught and motivated to focus on delivery of their specific projects. They are so busy with project details that they avoid getting drawn into the issues of other projects. In addition, they view other projects as competitors in the fight for budget. When executives support a process that identifies the right technology and business projects that jointly increase value for the company, staff can use the knowledge gained from this process to ensure maximum and appropriate use of technology in the future.

When we have brought business sponsors and project managers together to look at the business results from a number of projects, they experience a revelation as well as relief when the bigger picture finally emerges. Project managers then begin to recommend ways to increase efficient use of resources and optimize the budget across projects to realize business results. When executives see that important benefits and efficiencies are achieved by this integrated view of many projects, they have more confidence in meeting project goals and obtaining business results. By shifting the conversation to how value is being generated, the project becomes a vehicle for the business, not just technology implementation.

Strategic initiative management also allows companies to see the total costs associated with technology initiatives and to better understand the value and benefits they deliver. In many cases technical managers are charged with analyzing, evaluating, and explaining the costs and estimating benefits when business managers are not always encouraged to even learn how to do this. Sometimes the reverse is true. Business managers conduct project financial analysis more often than IT staff. The strategic initiative management process ensures that all managers develop an understanding of the business benefit and cost structure for technology investments. Then both business and technology managers are able to more effectively apply technology to their immediate operating responsibilities to produce business results. Through this process executives can obtain an organization-wide capability to deliver consistent short-term and long-term benefits from technology. In addition, we have found that when executives share the urgency and critical business information with staff, the company can exceed their initial goals. In this way staff can participate in running the business and generating value.

By launching strategic initiative management, a company is preparing to better manage technology investments. Now technology is part of every business function and activity, even though systems are not physically integrated. It is time to examine how your organization is obtaining value from these investments and creating new forms and levels of business performance. It is time for executives to take responsibility and accountability for the results from technology investments.

SUMMARY

Executives must be accountable for overseeing technology initiatives and securing the connection between technology investments and business objectives. Customers, investors, and staff are not concerned with the myths of technology; they want convenience, efficiency, and value. Executives must lead the shift across their organizations to a new way of thinking and acting that is based on real value and effective use of technology. Thinking strategically about technology and then using effective collaboration, decision making, measurement, and evaluation are the critical actions executives can use to help make this shift. Each and every initiative and project must have a clear value proposition statement that supports business objectives. When this shift occurs, executives can be confident that technology is more than a sunk cost; it is fulfilling its role as a powerful tool to improve business performance and competitiveness. It is time to move from basing technology decisions on hope and promise to basing them on measurable business benefits.

QUESTIONS FOR REFLECTION AND DISCUSSION

1. How do you ensure that strategic initiatives and objectives are communicated and considered when technology investments are made?

2. How do you link initiatives and projects to identify the overall effects on business performance?

3. How do you ensure that technology initiatives consistently deliver value?

4. How do you know the effects of technology investments on business performance?

5. How do you track and evaluate technology's impact on overall productivity, customer relationships, and realization of proposed financial benefits?

6. How can investment opportunities and risks in initiatives be identified before they are launched?

7. What tools and processes do you use to understand technology's broader effect on your entire business?

8. How do you know if your technology infrastructure is being fully leveraged for value by all initiatives?

9. What level of risk is your company willing to endure when considering technology investments?

NOTES

1. Cowley, M., and E. Domb. *Beyond Strategic Vision, Effective Corporate Action with Hoshin Planning*. Boston: Butterworth-Heinemann, 1997. Pages 99–

150 outline ways to review the plan and make individuals responsible across the company.

2. Murakami, K., "State Spends $40 Million for Nothing?," *Seattle Times,* 22 March 1997, p. 6.

3. Crane, D. B. "Seeing Solutions: Integrating Business, People and Technology to Generate Value." Workbook for graduate students by Project Concepts, Inc. Hayward, CA, 2000.

INDEX

About the Authors

DARLENE BARRIENTOS CRANE is President of PCI Crane Consulting.

MARGERY MAYER is CEO and Senior Management Consultant at Strategy & Process Experts, a consulting firm that bridges the gap between initiatives and results.